THE RUGBY WORLD CUP DIARIES

A referee's inside view

STUART DICKINSON

NEW
HOLLAND

First published in Australia in 2007 by
New Holland Publishers (Australia) Pty Ltd
Sydney • Auckland • London • Cape Town

1/66 Gibbes Street Chatswood NSW 2067 Australia
218 Lake Road Northcote Auckland New Zealand
86 Edgware Road London W2 2EA United Kingdom
80 McKenzie Street Cape Town 8001 South Africa

A record of this book is held at the National Library of Australia
ISBN: 9781741106473

Publishers: Fiona Schultz and Linda Williams
Managing Editor: Lliane Clarke
Editor: David McClintock
Designer: Tania Gomes
Production Assistant: Liz Malcolm
Printer: Griffin Press

10 9 8 7 6 5 4 3 2 1

Contents

I.

Introduction: A life of rugby

I have loved rugby for as long as I can remember. I began playing as a five-year-old with the Beecroft Junior Rugby Union Club and was immediately hooked. Like any kid I enjoyed the rough and tumble of the game and playing with my mates in a team. Those great games in the wet, when you scored a try and tested how far you could slide in the mud, were the best fun. From early on I became fascinated by the science and tactical nature of the game, a passion that remains to this day.

My father, John, a business manager, and my mother Helen, a registered nurse, provided the Saturday morning taxi service for me and my older brother Matt, who also played. Luckily, they both loved rugby.

I reached the U12s and began secondary school at Epping Boys High School. As a junior I played representative rugby with the Eastwood District Juniors and in State Championship and touring teams.

In 1980, when I was 12 years old, I was playing with the Beecroft Juniors in a seven-a-side competition at Pennant Hills Oval when the referee failed to turn up for the match. I volunteered to have a go at refereeing and I really liked it. There was plenty to learn but refereeing gave me with a unique insight and understanding of the game.

We had an exchange with the ACT juniors in the U12s and I found myself playing against Ricky Stuart—later a dual international and now Cronulla Rugby League coach. It was also the first time I saw and marvelled at the skills of the legendary David Campese. He was playing for Queanbeyan and scored a length of the field try, which he began from inside the in-goal area. He stepped and swerved his way through nearly every opposition player to eventually score under the posts.

At Epping Boys High School, I played as a flyhalf and fullback, starting in the U13s and moving through the age groups until I reached the First XV side in 1984 and 1985. As that was the senior open team, I played alongside my brother who was the Captain of our great 1985 side. That year we won the Zone Grand Final and played in the Waratah Shield Semi-final. Matt and I also played in the Northwest Metropolitan Zone First XV, the team that won the Zone Championship. It was a great year!

After high school, I played Third XV Colts Rugby for Eastwood in 1986 and 1987 and also managed to referee a few games. This was my final year as a player. I joined the NSW Police Force in 1987 and I knew that time away for training and the possibility of injury might have implications for the job. I also realised I wasn't going to achieve much more as a player. At the same time, I passionately believed I could be a Test referee.

Playing and refereeing

I do have to confess that being a young player and a referee at the same time was quite a challenge. There were many occasions when I questioned decisions during games that I knew were wrong, but I was put in my place and a life lesson was quickly learnt.

In those early years I began refereeing junior U8 and U9 matches on the half field at Somerville Oval, Eastwood under the great tutelage of Dick McGee and Mrs Robin Timmins. Twenty-seven years later I still have an ongoing association with Robin, as she is still involved in refereeing as the referee assistant at NSW Rugby Referees.

I moved through the grades with the District Association and found myself in the rather strange situation of refereeing age group teams that were only one year younger than me. Like playing, refereeing had become a great passion. It allowed me to be a better player and student of the game and even as a young kid I had a passionate belief that I could eventually referee at the highest level. It was that goal that kept me focused when other guys would point out that refereeing was 'for old blokes who couldn't play'.

My father John, who had a great involvement with the Eastwood District Juniors and was later honoured with Life Membership, was very much a part of my early refereeing career. He was my driver and chief supporter and no matter what the time or the location, we never ran late or got lost. He was always there with a smile and an encouraging word at the end of the game. I have no doubt that he gave me the tough mental edge required to be involved in refereeing at the highest level. Sadly he passed away on 22 January 2007 after a short but tough and brave fight with acute myeloid leukemia. We had many chats before he died and I certainly reminded him of the instrumental and greatly valued part that he played in my refereeing career.

In 1988 I made the move to the Sydney Rugby Referees Association, now known as the New South Wales Referees Association. This was a step up from junior rugby into the senior grade competition for suburban Sydney, known as 'Subbies Rugby'. The players were real men as tough as old boots and many as cunning as sewer rats. They were more than ready, willing and able to teach a young, fresh faced and inexperienced referee a few lessons in how to deal with rugby players on and off the field. I really enjoyed the whole experience and all the good and bad games that I had. I'm sure the players didn't enjoy my bad ones but that's life—we all make mistakes.

It was during this time that I first met Jim Middleton who was a former First Grade referee in Sydney. He was a referee coach and like a little Buddha he miraculously appeared from nowhere one afternoon to introduce himself and tell me he thought I was rough but had some promise. Over the years we have become great friends and he has been a trusted mentor instrumental in helping me learn the craft of refereeing.

In 1993, I was appointed to my initial First Grade match between Southern Districts and Norths at Forshaw Park. It was a great honour and was the start of a whole new learning curve. The First Grade competition was fierce and contained some of the greatest players Australian rugby has produced. I certainly learnt the trade quickly when I refereed the Randwick front row of Daly, Kearns and McKenzie who had also been the 1991 World Cup winning Wallaby front row. In the amateur era it was quite common to have up to 15 Wallabies out of the 30 players on the field. The challenge of rising to this level was a major motivator and I just wanted to learn more. I made plenty of mistakes but it was a great experience being able to go back to the bar after the match and speak to the players to improve my understanding and knowledge of the game.

The game of rugby union became professional in 1996 and the Super 12 provincial competition between Australian, New Zealand and South Africa began.

Along with fellow Australian referees, Andrew Cole, Wayne Erickson, Peter Marshall and Scott Young, I was appointed to officiate in these matches. The five of us became semi-professional by signing a part-time contract and in 1997 we became the first full-time rugby union referees in Australia. With Russell Trotter as our ARU referee manager we entered the unknown but exciting world of professional rugby refereeing. It was the most successful time in the history of Australian rugby refereeing, as there had never been five Australian Test referees at the one time. As a group we were able to keep raising the standard of Australian refereeing. I have now refereed 61 Super 12/14 Rugby matches including four semi-finals.

My first Test match

I was appointed to my first Test match in 1997. It was a RWC qualifying match between Papua New Guinea and Tahiti in Port Moresby. My wife, Fiona, and one of my best mates, Wayne Borland, came to watch and they tell me it was 45°C in the shade. The match was won by PNG, 97–0. It was just such a great honour to represent Australia and I thought back to all the people who have helped the game and all the sacrifices they, and I, have had to make.

I have refereed 36 Test matches. At the 1999 Rugby World Cup in Wales I refereed the quarter-final playoff between Argentina and Ireland. Argentina beat their more fancied opponents and when I blew full-time the Argentinean flyhalf, Felipe Contemponi, grabbed and hugged the nearest player to him. It wasn't actually a player—it was me. I tried to get out of the embrace as quickly as possible as it wasn't a good look! I was still fined 40 pounds in our referees' and officials' 'Kangaroo Court'. The 'Kangaroo Court' is held at the end of the tournament and we award each other spoof awards. It is a great opportunity for us to have lots of laughs at each other's expense, as well as raising money for charity.

Refereeing at the 2003 Rugby World Cup in Australia was great because I was able to referee at home. To maintain neutrality we obviously cannot referee matches Australia plays in, so we usually ply our trade away from home. In 2003, I refereed South Africa v Georgia at the Sydney Football Stadium and it was a magnificent experience. My wife and family were there and the game was a great occasion. When Georgia scored a try the noise of 38,000 sounded more like a full house of 80,000 at Millennium Stadium in Cardiff.

The greatest part of refereeing is the involvement in the game and the challenge that it provides. You are making decisions in a challenging and at times hostile environment and you learn a lot about yourself. I call it the best seat in the house, as you are only metres away from the action. The challenge is all about growth as a person and how you cope with both constructive and negative criticism. Many people question our sanity but I love the opportunity it provides to self-evaluate, set goals and consistently improve performance levels. Another aspect I enjoy is the great opportunity that world travel provides. The chance to experience the many differing landscapes, cultures and people around the world is a humbling experience. I have managed to see the best and worst this world has to offer and it's enabled me to both grow and learn as a person. I always think how lucky I am to be able to be involved in this great game.

Life off the rugby field

Looking back, there were a number of influences outside rugby that helped shape my desire to become and improve as a top-level referee. I have been very lucky with the moments, places and people that have helped define and direct my life. I am forever grateful to my parents, my brother and sister, friends, work mates and my wife and children who have all played a major role in my life.

I had a wonderful childhood growing up in Beecroft in the north of Sydney. I was the youngest of three children. My sister Linda is three years older and my brother Mathew is 18 months older. Much time was spent playing in the bush and the creeks that surrounded the houses near ours—out after breakfast, back for lunch so Mum could check you were still alive, and then home before dark.

I finished high school at Epping Boys High in 1985. My time there was amazing—I had so many opportunities. Sport was obviously a major interest for me. Ian Dundon, Geoff Wing, Col Harris, Mary Lopez, Terry Chapman and many other teachers there were selfless and tireless in their efforts to educate inside and outside of the classroom. Many of them remain friends to this day. They expected us to 'strive to achieve', just as the school motto stated. Mary Lopez helped form the school rugby choir and this allowed us to sing at various venues while on a rugby tour of New Zealand as well as perform at the opening of the Sydney Entertainment Centre.

After working as a trainee manager with a textile company for a year, I found a job with East-West Airlines in their reservations department. This was a great job with great people and I had a lot of fun. From booking flights to dealing with trivial complaints, I learnt some skills in dealing with and managing people and situations.

A gun at my head

I joined the NSW Police Service in 1987. After completing three months training at the NSW Police Academy in Goulburn I was posted to Ryde Police Station as a general duties officer. As a Police Officer I rapidly learned some important life skills, as the decisions you make and situations you face have the potential to change lives forever. These life skills are massively important in refereeing, as they play a major role in determining how you cope with adversity and deal with human relations.

After a couple of years dealing with traffic accidents, domestic disputes, theft offences and so on, I joined the Chatswood District Special Operations Group. This unit was established to reduce the number of property thefts in the district. It was a great group with brilliant bosses in Ron Daly and Ken Lawrence, two experienced policeman who expected excellence and gave unwavering support.

On 4 September 1991 one incident I was involved in changed my life, although I didn't know it at the time. I was patrolling with my partner, Craig Kirkland. There had been a number of robberies in the area and at around 2am in the morning I saw someone acting suspiciously near a pub.

I left the police car and walked over to have a look while my partner drove around the block into the adjoining car park. There was a brick wall that ran beside the wall of the pub which provided an alcove area where the air conditioning units were. I heard a noise and went to investigate. The rear part of the alcove was in the dark and as I wandered in a person stepped out of the dark into the lit area where I was standing. I could sense trouble just by his demeanour—it is hard to explain but a copper just knows it deep in his gut. As he stepped out he pulled his hand out from behind his back and levelled a .38 revolver at my stomach.

Trouble had definitely arrived and I wasn't waiting for an introduction or a bullet. I grabbed his hand and gun and jammed my right middle finger between the trigger and the trigger guard so I could stop him discharging the gun. It then became a life and death struggle between us—I could feel the trigger jamming on my finger as he tried to fire the gun. It must have been a rehearsal for refereeing as he was also calling me all the names under the sun at the same time as questioning my ability to do my job!

We struggled out into the car park at some pace where I struck my back on a bollard—but I wasn't giving in. Craig was getting worried when he couldn't find me, and then suddenly he saw us emerge into the light. Although he couldn't see a gun, from his position more then 50 metres away he could tell it was a life and death struggle. He got quite a surprise when he arrived to help me and found the bloke had a gun. With Craig's help I managed to handcuff him and bring him to the ground, calling for backup. Craig opened the chamber of the gun and we saw it was fully loaded with six bullets. I suppose I shouldn't have been that surprised because the crook did keep telling me he was going to kill me but, as any good copper knows, crooks are always telling lies.

The crowning glory and comic relief of that night came in the form of the Duty Officer who had raced to the scene with lights flashing and sirens blaring. When he pulled into the driveway of the pub at high speed he failed to see the chain across the driveway—he soon heard it though when the chain ripped the entire siren and light system off the roof of the police car.

Craig Kirkland and I received the Commissioner's Valour Award for our efforts. I see the whole incident as a positive, life changing experience. Those sorts of experiences really make you have a look at yourself and realise the importance of family and friends. I felt as though I'd faced a major test and passed it.

In 1993, after six years with the Police Service, I felt it was time to move on. I was feeling frustrated with the way the police culture was changing and wanted to take on some new challenges, including having a crack at taking my refereeing to the highest level.

In 1997 I started refereeing full-time with Andrew Cole, Wayne Erickson, Peter Marshall and Scott Young. I signed the first professional refereeing contract with the Australian Rugby Union in 1997. As the ARU national referees panel we were in the vanguard of change for refereeing. As rugby moved into the professional era, the demands on referees intensified. Higher levels of fitness were required to deal with the increased speed and intensity of the game. The introduction of video referees and increased use of technology for pre and post-game analysis meant decisions were under intense scrutiny.

The late 1990s were a triumphant time for Australian rugby refereeing. All five national referees were selected for the 1999 Rugby World Cup in Wales. After Wayne's retirement the four of us remaining were selected for the 2003 RWC in Australia. Unfortunately Scott was injured during fitness testing and couldn't take part. They were all outstanding Test referees and it was a great privilege and honour to have worked with them. Now I am enjoying different relationships with them. Peter is my boss as National Referees Manager and Wayne, Andrew and Scott are involved with the coaching and selecting of referees at a national level.

Of course, one of the biggest influences on my life has been marrying and starting a family with my wife Fiona. I'm forever grateful to my great schoolmate, Dale Sessions, who introduced us in 1992. We were married at St Patrick's Church in East Gosford in November 1995 and have three children, Michael born in 2001 and twin girls Emily and Isabella born in 2003.

It has been an interesting journey from when I first picked up the ball and ran with it as a five-year-old to now as I prepare to referee at my third World Cup.

II.

Preparing for

the 2007 Rugby World Cup

I am the only Australian referee at the 2007 World Cup, which makes it very different to the other tournaments. Paul Marks from Queensland will be there as a touch judge, but he will return home at the completion of the pool rounds. Ian Scotney, our National Referee Selector, will also be going to the tournament as an IRB Performance Reviewer. Ian also attended the 2003 World Cup in the same capacity and it is a fitting recognition of Ian's pioneering work over many years in improving referee coaching and assessment at the international level.

I am very proud and honoured to be one of three Australians who will take part. The fact that Australia has just one referee here certainly doesn't mean that Australian refereeing is on the decline. We have just come to the end of a very successful cycle and are now in the rebuilding phase with a number of referees coming through. Matt Goddard, James Leckie, Paul Marks, and Brett Bowden are all Test referees and part of our national squad. A number of newer faces are also making their way through so the depth is good. It is just a matter of building their experience. I expect to see more Aussie refs at the next World Cup in New Zealand.

A tough selection process

The referee and touch judge appointments for RWC 2007 come after an exhaustive process. We are always being watched! Selection panels at domestic, provincial and international levels continually monitor national referees' performances. The International Rugby Board Referee Selection Committee—David Pickering (Chairman), Paddy O'Brien (International Referee Manager), Kevin Bowring, Tappe Henning, Bob Francis, Stephen Hilditch and Michel Lamoulie—receive reports from the selection panels as well as reports from Selectors and Performance Reviewers at particular matches. A database of all this information is then used to help make international appointments.

In the current professional era, elite panel referees are usually made up of referees who have officiated at a European Cup or Super 14 level. These are high standard competitions and consistently provide matches that are the closest possible to that of Test match rugby. The selectors can gauge the progress and standards of the referees when they can review them in this environment.

The selection process for Test matches is carried out by the IRB Referee Selection Committee three to four times per year. Committee members are in constant dialogue and Paddy O'Brien is always providing referees with feedback—good, bad or ugly.

As a referee, your performance is officially reviewed at every match you officiate, whether it is as a referee, touch judge or television match official (video referee). The review process is carried out by either a Selector or Performance Reviewer attending the match. A Selector prepares a report based on their observations at the ground and then clarifies any issues with a review of the game on DVD. Their report is a qualitative assessment of the referee's performance in four areas: game description, management performance, technical performance, and areas for improvement.

A performance reviewer conducts a quantitative analysis by logging referee non-compliance to an agreed set of criteria. The relevant selection committees at both the provincial (European Cup and Super 14) and international (IRB) levels use this information to help them select referees for matches. There is always a furious unofficial debate with lots of people giving their opinion on your performance. You can't take it to heart, as it will ultimately affect your performance. The more experience you gain helps you to manage this better. It is important to build the support networks that can give you positive and constructive feedback. As an individual the most important aspect to achieving growth is that you are prepared to accept your supporters and reviewers opinions and be able to honestly 'take a look in the hall of mirrors' when you review this information. When you can do this, you are then in a position to learn. That is the cornerstone to growth as an individual.

From my perspective I look at what I can control, and that is my performance on and off the field. I also keep aspiring to the philosophy, 'Don't give them a reason not to pick you'.

Preparing my body for the Cup

The ARU, as part of its ongoing development program for referees, employs a trainer/conditioner who writes and conducts training programs. In Sydney, Matt Donohoe is our trainer. Due to our extended travel requirements and virtual year-round season he maintains a balance between the running, weights and cross training elements required to keep us fit and fresh.

The IRB conducted our pre RWC fitness testing in June 2007 at the Sydney Academy of Sport in Sydney's Narrabeen. The testing requires us to complete a set of standard tests to determine whether we are maintaining or improving our fitness levels. There is no pass/fail mark and you are essentially competing against yourself.

Once the fitness tests were concluded I began preparing for the two Test matches that I refereed before the RWC—NZ v France in Auckland on 2 June, and NZ v South Africa in Christchurch on 14 July.

The aim of my physical preparation was to lighten the load on the legs leading up to those matches. I did one running session per week as well as cross training with swimming, exercise bike classes and weight training.

I refereed some First XV colts (U20) and First XV suburban rugby matches to keep my mind and body ticking over and to fine tune and practice some positional and technical matters. I made a conscious choice to only referee matches that did not involve the new IRB experimental law variations which were being trialled in some Australian competitions. I believe it would have been too difficult to master two sets of laws over a short period and that it would unduly affect my performance on the field.

After the Test matches were over I concentrated mainly on long distance running sessions as well as exercise bike classes in order to build a strong aerobic base for the tournament. We have to maintain an excellent blend of both aerobic and anaerobic fitness levels in order to be in the right positions to make good decisions.

I also kept up with a weights program that is designed to increase muscle strength and endurance as opposed to building or hypertrophy of major muscles. This is achieved by doing numerous sets at a lower weight. Another important part of any training program is maintaining flexibility and core stability. As athletes we need to maintain strength in the abdominal muscles so that they can support the other muscles required for running. I keep flexible through Pilates and stretching exercises.

New Zealand v France: 2 June 2007

I was well prepared for this game, but it didn't turn out as I had hoped. There were positive and negative comments about my performance, but when I did a postmatch review I found I had made decisions that were out of character and wrong.

The first few decisions in the first seven minutes were not quite right. I played advantage to France for a knock-on by New Zealand and a French player kicked the ball up field about 20 metres. I looked ahead through the maze of black jerseys and saw no New Zealander there, at the same time I saw a French player leading the race for the ball so I called advantage over. Suddenly Dan Carter, the NZ flyhalf, appeared out of nowhere and picked up the ball. He must have blended into the background or was hidden by a jersey but I had already called advantage over. Wrong decision—no advantage to France—I should have come back for a scrum to them. I then penalised the French No 9 for being offside at a ruck when it should have been play on. Next, I gave a free kick against France for closing the gap at a lineout—I could have managed it a different way by letting NZ just throw in the ball and see if the French infringement had an effect. If not, play on and talk to them at the next lineout: if so, then free kick. So much for striving to achieve some form of excellence—not!

NZ won the game by a large margin and while some of my decisions were wrong they didn't cost France the game. As a referee you prepare as best you can to make the correct decisions and if you do get them wrong then you just hope they don't cost a side victory.

As a referee, you make between 4000 and 6000 decisions in a match, so it is understandable that you sometimes make errors of judgment. You try not to, but hell, like players who drop the ball, we're only human.

NZ v France 2 June 2007	
Auckland	
New Zealand	42
France	11

The Second Test and Bernard Laporte

For the Second Test between New Zealand and France on 9 June I was appointed touch judge and reserve referee. Craig Joubert from South Africa was referee. On the Friday evening Craig was due to meet Bernard Laporte, the French coach, at our hotel for a prematch meeting and he enquired as to whether I would like to accompany him. I declined, as it is always my position that if you have refereed the team the week before then it is unfair to the referee and coach if you are there—they will obviously want to discuss elements of that match. I asked Craig to let Bernard know that I wanted to catch up with him at the ground to have a quick chat and apologise for a couple of the decisions that I had got wrong.

Some time later Craig rang to let me know that Bernard was happy to have a chat if I had the time. I went upstairs to meet Bernard in the foyer of the hotel. Bernard was accompanied by Dave Ellis, France's defence and tactical coach, and the video analyst who had a laptop. We moved to where we were away from the general public, or so I thought.

The meeting was very cordial and I began by apologising to Bernard and the French team for the incorrect decisions. He accepted that apology and then had the video analyst play some clips of NZ players who, in his opinion, were offside at the ruck/maul and had interfered with the game. During the discussion Bernard was obviously upset but at no time did he raise his voice. I attempted to tell him that I agreed the players were in offside positions but that they were not having an effect on play. This went round in circles for a while and I knew there was no sense in continuing to labour the point.

Bernard then made a number of comments that essentially implied that I would not referee his team again and that he would be in touch with Paddy O'Brien about my performance. I shook his hand and we all went our own way. I was concerned about the comments but at the same time I also understood that the French team and the coach were under pressure.

The French are very passionate about their rugby, which is great for the game, but I did think that Bernard had crossed a line. It was my intention to let it die down and then have a quiet word with Paddy O'Brien the following week so that it could be dealt with in-house.

After saying good-bye I got in the lift. Another gentlemen entered and made a comment relating to the incident. At the time I just said something like 'that's life and the sun will come up tomorrow'. I now know he was Trevor McKewen from the *Sunday Star-Times* newspaper as an article appeared the next day about the 'incident'. I received a number of calls and great support from Peter Marshall and the Australian Rugby Union. I also didn't add any fuel to the fire by commenting to the press. It wouldn't have been in the game's or anyone's best interest. Paddy made contact and I submitted a report to the IRB who then forwarded it onto the French Federation. Bernard replied by sending a letter written in French. As it is his native language I didn't really have too much of a problem with that. He apologised and as far as I am concerned that is the end of the matter. I'm happy to see him and chat to him again at any time.

NZ v France: 9 June 2007	
Wellington	
New Zealand	61
France	10

New Zealand v South Africa: 14 July 2007

This was a classic Test match with the South Africans staying close until the final 12 minutes when New Zealand scored three tries. They had a team described by the media as a 'B' team due to injuries and first choice players being rested for the RWC.

I prepared well for this match and it was always my expectation that, with NZ having made seven changes and the South Africans having their pride and integrity questioned by the media, it would be a close and physical match. The South Africans showed great courage and New Zealand hung in there to eventually run away at the end.

I was really pleased with my decision making in that it was clear, concise and consistent. There are always little things to work on at the edges to keep improving but I know it was a huge step up from the previous NZ v France match.

NZ v SA: 14 July 2007	
Christchurch	
New Zealand	33
South Africa	6

I have now done all I can to prepare for the 2007 Rugby World Cup. I now have to make sure that I cross the Ts and dot the Is during my pool round matches, control my part and hopefully put myself in the frame for selection for matches later on.

Prematch television coverage

Mike Heaton, Channel Ten's Rugby World Cup producer, asked me to help out with some prematch coverage so on 3 August I met the Channel Ten team at Manly Oval to film some segments about the laws of the game to help educate both novices and avid fans. Ben Darwin, former Wallaby prop and now Channel Ten commentator for the Cup, and players from the Manly team helped out on a cold and drizzly afternoon. I hope this will add some value to their coverage and help the cause of the referee as we are always striving to educate the rugby public about our role.

In August I went to the Channel Ten studios in Pyrmont Sydney for the filming of the first panel show to launch their coverage of the 2007 Rugby World Cup.

It was hosted by Bill Woods and Rupert McCall with former Wallabies Ben Tune and Ben Darwin as the expert rugby commentators. They are terrific guys and, with an obvious rapport between them all, they should develop into a great commentary team. They are really unlucky that they will be working from a studio on the Champs Élysées, which will be known as the Heineken Bar. While IRB rules won't allow referees to appear on any shows or be involved with newspapers, I will certainly be taking them up on their offer to come down and visit and share a quiet 'orange juice'. The taping took a few hours. It was a great opportunity to highlight the role of the match officials as part of whole RWC.

Leaving Sydney for France

Wednesday 29 August: The last training session in Sydney was a boxing session with the other national squad referees at the NSW Waratahs' new gym with our trainer Matt Donohoe. It started at 6am so I was up at 5.

Of course we were hitting pads held by someone as opposed to boxing in a ring. Matt's training programs, enthusiasm and attitude of excellence have played a big part in keeping the squad fit and motivated. I really wanted to have a last blowout as the next 24 hours or so would be full of 'gentle rest' at 30,000 feet. Although I am not a 'fight fan' I gained an immediate respect for the fitness and strength levels required by boxers when we started this type of training nearly 10 years ago. Today's session was a typical Donohoe special with plenty of hard hitting.

An hour and a quarter later with limp arms and a feeling of satisfaction, I headed home to finish packing and see my kids for the last time until the end of the Cup. My wife, Fiona, will be joining me for a week from 10 October. That will be great, especially for her, as she has had the grand total of three days away from our kids in six years. I don't think any words can do justice to Fi and the sacrifices she has had to make so that I can pursue my dreams.

Leaving the family for extended periods is definitely the hardest thing about refereeing as a job. On the other hand, I get to spend a great deal of time with them when I am at home. I have even become an honorary member of the mothers' groups as I take Michael to school and hang out before school starting and every Tuesday I take Emily and Bella to playgroup.

Whenever I travel to referee I try not to lose sight of the fact that it is a great honour and privilege to be selected to represent your country. I feel a sense of relief that the waiting is over and I can get on the plane and put plans into action for what I expect to be a most enjoyable and challenging tournament

The first leg of the flight to Kuala Lumpur took about seven hours. I always stay awake during that leg to Europe as I find it is the best way to acclimatise to the time difference. By the time I get back on the plane for the next 13-hour leg I'm very tired and I sleep for eight hours or more. Of course, a little sleeping tablet always helps. Travelling business class gives you plenty of room and being able to lie down in a bed is magnificent.

Touchdown in Paris

Thursday 30 August: The plane touched down in Paris at 6.45am. I'm pretty sure there is now a divot in the runway as it was the hardest landing I have ever experienced. I felt rested and refreshed which was very handy because when I approached the passport control area there was a huge lineup. Three planes had just landed and customs had put on a grand total of three staff. Finally through customs, I was met by a liaison officer from the French RWC organising committee.

The airport was awash with RWC flags and there is no doubt that the French are determined to put on a spectacle. In fact, given that rugby is most popular in the south of the country it was terrific to see and feel the vibe on first arrival. I was then driven into Paris in brilliant morning sunshine. Paris in summer, how magnificent! And people keep saying

'Why would you want to be a referee?'.

Peak hour traffic meant a scenic and slow journey and at 10am we pulled up outside the Novotel Hotel Gare de Lyon, the referee base and home for the next two months. The hotel was selected specifically for its proximity to the Gare de Lyon railway station, one of the hubs for the fast train (TGV) network that will transport us to and from various locations. I wandered into the hotel to be greeted by the South African referees—Mark Lawrence, Marius Jonker and Craig Joubert—and our boss Paddy O'Brien. Unfortunately for Craig his bags had managed to take a detour to parts unknown and there was no booking for him at the hotel. The rest of us checked in and proceeded back down to meet Paddy and pick up our tournament kit. There was a massive amount of good quality gear. The only downside is that I am not sure how the white shorts and socks will look on my untanned legs!

Off the field, humour is a great part of refereeing and you can't afford to take yourself too seriously. Paddy O'Brien has a quick wit and a great sense of humour, so it didn't take long for Craig to be targeted when he joined us in the team room. Craig was trying to locate his kit when Paddy remarked 'wasn't missing luggage and no room a big enough hint'.

It was then back to the room with goodies in tow to pack a smaller bag to take to Tignes on Friday for our three-day team building camp.

The hotel has a lap pool so I did a swimming recovery session to refresh and stretch the body after the long flight. Then out for a walk into the sunshine with fellow referees—Mark, Craig, Marius and also Jonathan Kaplan. We ventured along the Seine and found a café near Notre Dame.

I was really looking forward to the next day and my first trip on the TGV and the chance to see the magnificent French countryside.

Team building in Tignes

Friday 31 August: The pleasures of jetlag dawned when I woke at 3.30am. The best remedy is to grab a book and start reading. I managed to get back to sleep about an hour later and woke at 8am feeling fresh.

The northern hemisphere referees arrived this morning, completing the on-field match officials' team. We all met at the team room for refitting of the suits and other clothing. The atmosphere was lighthearted and you can feel the 'referee family' atmosphere clicking in. The team has a really good vibe with everyone taking the opportunity to catch up on personal and family news. There was, of course, the mandatory humour that helps bind any team.

Today we set off on the five-hour journey to the ski resort of Tignes in southern France. Before we left we had a group photo taken on the steps of the massive Hotel courtyard.

Tony Spreadbury, one of the funniest men you will ever meet, put his England Rugby bag in front of the group to help remind us that England are still World Champions. Bragging rights were quickly dismissed along with the bag which magically flew some distance.

We boarded the TGV in first class—we are certainly being well looked after—and at 2.20pm we left Gare de Lyon bound for Chambery. I was looking forward to this trip as I have not travelled on the TGV or seen a lot of the countryside of southern France. I was sitting with Wayne Barnes from England who is attending his first Rugby World Cup and will referee four games. Wayne is a barrister and at only 29 is probably the youngest referee in the team. He is a clever man and a very good referee and will have a great career.

The French countryside was spectacular with green rolling hills and quaint little villages dotted along the way. As we neared Chambery the sight of the alpine mountains with their wispy low hanging clouds was truly remarkable.

From Chambery most of the group travelled by bus. However, Paddy O'Brien, Tony Spreadbury and Jonathan Kaplan travelled by car with our liaison person. Paddy can be excused because he is in charge but the group left on the bus decided that—at our 'kangaroo court' later in the tournament—fines would have to be imposed on the other two for taking a 'private tour'.

The trip took about two hours and while everyone was tired the scenery was breathtaking. On the way we passed through Albertville, home of the 1992 Winter Olympics. We then made the steep climb up to Tignes at altitude 2100m. Tignes is located in the Tarentaise Valley and the beauty of this place is incredible. Massive mountains with sheer drops from the side of the road had everyone mesmerised. A fear of heights had some of the guys moving away from the bus windows though.

Once at Tignes we had a lovely meal at a local restaurant. Speciality dishes of the region are mainly based on potatoes and melted cheese (fondue/raclette), accompanied by an array of different hams (tartiflette).

At dinner, Paul Honiss made a special presentation to Tony Spreadbury. Paul had refereed the opening game of RWC 2003 and Tony will to do the same at this RWC. Paul had a special trophy made with the names of the referees who have refereed the opening match engraved onto it. I thought that was a magnificent gesture and it was well received by the entire referee team.

Mental preparation

Saturday 1 September: What a magnificent day, clear blue skies and some light cloud drifting over the mountain ranges to make the scenery look like a picture postcard.

A number of press agencies are travelling with us, including the boys who film for the International Rugby Board's *Total Rugby* show. They had some interesting filming during the earpiece moulding session. When we are officiating we wear communication equipment to stay in contact with other match officials and also provide a link of our voices to the host broadcaster. To make the earpiece we have a type of putty squeezed into our ear. At first it feels as though it has gone halfway through your brain. It takes a few minutes to set and the whole lot is then removed from your ear and a mould is formed. The mould is used to make perfect fitting earpieces that we'll receive next week.

A few of us went down to an area that has tennis courts and a beach soccer field. Paul Honiss flogged me at tennis and then we had a kick of the balls on the sand soccer field. We played 'crossbar challenge' where you kick the ball from the halfway line and attempt to hit the crossbar. Simon McDowell (Ireland), Federico Cuesta (Argentina), Rhys Jones (Wales) our video analyst and I played. It was great fun. We are certainly relaxing and getting right away from rugby which is the purpose of the trip. Performance on the field is probably 90 per cent mental and preparing a great state of mind is helped by getting away and shutting off from rugby for a while.

In the afternoon our group met up with the Stade Francais rugby team, who were in the village on a training camp. We caught the funicular up to the mountain region known as Glacier La Grande Motte. This was one of the most spectacular sights I have ever seen with 360 degree views of this most majestic and awe inspiring mountain formation. We then caught a cable car to the top of the ski run area and the view back down was breathtaking.

There was a large amount of icy snow on the slopes and there were lots of kids and adults skiing. At 3600 metres we were a bit short of breath, but that was forgotten when we had our group photo and the Stade Francais boys starting throwing snowballs at us. There is nothing like a good snow fight. For an Australian it is hard to believe you can make snowballs on the first day of autumn. Our press friends from *Total Rugby* were filming the snow fight and I'm sure the footage will be great!

Sunday 2 September: Our last day at Tignes and the end of a fantastic period of relaxation before to the start of the tournament. Paul Marks (Australia), Malcolm Changleng (Scotland), Simon McDowell (Ireland), Craig Joubert (South Africa) and I played nine holes of golf. The course was particularly hilly and, combined with the altitude, we found that it was a good workout for the lungs and the legs. The guys from *Total Rugby* caught up with us and did some filming and we had a lot of very funny moments.

The *Total Rugby* guys also wanted to conduct an interview with me. For Australian referees media interest is a bit of a novelty as we tend to be more anonymous compared to our colleagues from countries such as New Zealand or South Africa where rugby is the top sport and referees have a high profile.

After lunch we set off on the drive down the mountain to Chambery to catch the TGV to Paris. The return home was uneventful but the TGV is a world-class service. A couple of young boys came through the cabin and wanted all of us to sign autographs for them. They were clearly delighted and it is always nice to be able to put a smile on the faces of kids who love the game.

Monday is the start of our official duties. We will be addressed by Mr Syd Millar, Chairman of the International Rugby Board, and Mr Mike Miller, Rugby World Cup Managing Director. We then break into syndicate groups discussing the various technical areas and aspects of the game. Tuesday will follow a similar pattern with discussion of technical and game issues followed by a meeting with all the team coaches.

It is so important to plan ahead so you are not in a rush and you don't put any added pressure on yourself by not being properly prepared. In order for things to go well on the field you must tick off the boxes regarding the various processes required. If your processes aren't right then you can seriously affect the outcome and in our business we expect our outcomes and performance on the field to be excellent.

I will be a touch judge for the opening match, France v Argentina, on Friday night. On Saturday night I will be television match official for the England v USA match in Lens and on Sunday I will be the No 4 official (substitute controller) for the South Africa v Samoa match in Paris.

The No 4 and 5 role is where a match official is assigned to look after each team and ensure that substitutes are made through that official who then talks to the referee at the appropriate stoppage to make sure he is aware and in fact allows that substitution to occur. Each team fills out a card with the players numbers as an official record and the 4 and

5 make sure the laws are adhered to in respect of the correct number and type of substitutions allowed. This could be for an injury or blood bin and this process must be followed to ensure equity and adherence to the laws of the game. The No 4 and 5 officials are also responsible for ensuring the players warm up in their correct area and that the team medical people and runners also adhere to the rules.

The first day of serious work

Monday 3 September: Here we go! We're into the tournament proper with the first day of serious work. I started early with a 6am training session on the treadmill followed by a swim recovery session.

Today was the first of two days scheduled for meetings to discuss the many and varied aspects pertaining to our refereeing of the tournament. At 9am, Paddy O'Brien officially welcomed and congratulated the group on their selection and set the scene by stating that it was his expectation that 'enjoyment' be a key component of our time here. He ran through a variety of logistical issues, then Chairman of the IRB, Dr Syd Millar, officially welcomed us.

Dr Millar outlined his views of the tournament and what was expected of us. He produced the following facts: four billion television viewers; two million spectators; and RWC is the biggest sporting event in 2007. These facts blew me away and it was a reality check that you were in the middle of something so big and so special. He spoke about the 'Charter of the Game' and that the role of the referee in this tournament was to apply the laws of the game and create a fair contest so that all participants can showcase Rugby Union to the world over the next seven weeks. The tournament was being hosted in a magnificent country and would be judged by what occurred on the field and we should enjoy the experience. His demeanour and delivery were exceptionally positive and it left me in no doubt that the IRB would be very supportive of us as a group. That support is crucial to a positive mindset for the referees so that we can do our job properly.

Paddy stressed the importance of the need for us to be accurate but to also take into account 'materiality' when making decisions. 'Materiality' means—did your decision have an effect on the playing of the game? The emphasis was placed on achieving 'equal refereeing'. We must ensure that we are continually looking at both teams and not focusing on the actions of one in particular situations. This is especially applicable at the breakdown or 'tackle area' where there has been a trend to focus more on the defending side while allowing the attacking team more latitude.

How players enter the 'tackle area' is crucial to the contest for possession and we must ensure this contest occurs. The other discussion was about players standing offside and in front of their team mates thereby interfering with the opposition at the ruck and maul phase. This has become a blight on the game and strict instructions were given to pay attention to this problem and eradicate the practice.

Another contentious area has been the new scrum engagement

procedure and various ways that referees have been calling the sequence. It was changed this year, due to safety concerns from collapsed scrums, and became a four stage call of 'Crouch–Touch–Pause–Engage'. There was confusion in relation to the cadence of the call and whether it should be four separate words or whether 'Touch' and 'Pause' would be called with no gap between them as 'TouchPause'. It sounds trivial but it is crucial for the teams to have consistency so that they can practise and play correctly. The 12 referees met and agreed that there would be four deliberate and separate calls in sequential order.

We then worked through the areas of scrum feeds, maul, lineout, knock-on and tackle/ruck. This forum was designed to ensure that all match officials are in sync as this is crucial for consistency in decision making. Negative trends in these areas of the game were identified and discussed and a plan made for their solution. In the lineout, throwing teams have been stepping across toward the opposition and interfering with the other team's ability to jump and contest possession. We made a decision that we would manage this by first stopping the throw and requesting they not to do it, followed by a free kick if they don't touch another player, then a penalty kick if there was contact causing obstruction.

All of these discussions and solutions were based on the premise that we were not going to overreact and penalise everything. Quite the opposite, the solution is to manage it by recognising that the actions are liable to sanction and if they have an effect then apply that sanction.

This World Cup should be won by the team who plays the best and wins the contest. Our job is to provide the platform where that fair contest can take place and then it becomes a matter for the teams how even the contest will be.

Touch judging was also discussed with Bob Francis leading the meeting. It was the selector's view that there needs to be a massive improvement in the accuracy, consistency and teamwork of touch judges. The pre-game briefing is crucial to making sure that all participants are aware of their role on the day and that the 'team of three' functions as a unit. The basic premise is that touch judges should only call situations that are 'clear and obvious'.

The tone of the day was clear—we need to make sure we are setting a standard of excellence and doing our very best to achieve it. We will make mistakes but the crucial aspect is that we are consciously and consistently trying to achieve that high standard.

Player dissent was discussed and there is no doubt we do not want our game to follow soccer and other sports where it is commonplace and accepted that match officials will be subjected to dissent. There has been a worrying trend where players show open disregard for decisions by gesticulating toward or questioning referees. The IRB is clear that Rugby will not go down this path. All the RWC teams were sent a letter that clearly stated that any form of dissent is not acceptable and there will be a zero tolerance policy. Referees were instructed to take immediate and firm action if players engage in such actions. Each situation will be viewed on its merits and zero tolerance can range from telling a player to be quiet through to the ultimate sanction of sending a player off. I think the gentle reminder from the IRB will have the desired effect as there is so much at stake in the tournament that coaches will remind their players of their responsibilities and we referees won't have any issues to deal with.

The final discussion was about the television match official (TMO) and the protocol relating to its use. This was a very spirited debate with many views aired. The interesting point about all the debates is that we are always relating our points of view back to what is good for the game and how it allows the players to express themselves within those laws. The common cry about referees is that we are aiming to stifle the game when the opposite is definitely the case. Coaches and players will always come up with new and varied ways to play the game but our role is to ensure that this play is within the spirit and the laws of the game.

The TMO debate centred on whether we should go outside the protocol in order to get the 'correct' decision. At the moment the protocol states that referees can refer decisions that are 'in the act' of scoring, and with tries that refer to the last movement before scoring—such as the dive at the line. Our dilemma is that what happens if, for example, a player puts his foot on the line three or four steps before diving for that try?

The correct decision, according to the protocol, is that you cannot refer it to the TMO. This current protocol is in place because our game is fluid and the question is about how far back you go and how much time this takes. The IRB council members had decided that the protocol must be adhered to and so be it.

We re-confirmed the two calls that referees will make relating to tries: 'Can you give me any reason why I cannot award a try?' and 'Has a try been scored?'. The former relates to the fact that on many occasions you are 99.9 per cent sure a try has been scored and it should stand, unless the TMO can give you concrete evidence why it can't be awarded.

The classic example is the rolling maul where one team has it clearly at the back and they go over the goal line and the ball disappears into the bodies. Both teams will be happy to both accept and concede a try as each knows the same test or premise will be applied equally. The joys of being a decision maker.

The principles of rugby

Tuesday 4 September: Today's meeting began with Stephen Hilditch, one of the four selectors, giving a briefing on the selection process for the tournament. He re-confirmed that form was the major influence on selection and no-one was ruled out of selection for the knock-out stage of the tournament. The selectors had reviewed and simplified their performance report to focus on assessing referee performance. The expectation was that we were selected as the 12 best referees in the world and should be making the correct decisions. Therefore, the report would not be overly descriptive and the game description would concentrate on the degree of challenge in each match as well as technical and management issues. The degree of challenge is crucial to assessing referee performance. Most people think that games between first tier teams, such as England and South Africa, provide the greatest challenge but that is not always the case. Sometimes when two second tier teams meet in the pool stage they regard the match as their 'World Cup Final'. The skill level may not be as high but the intensity and pressure is enormous, which can make it as challenging a match to referee as a first tier match.

The next presentation was from Corris Thomas, a former Welsh Test referee, who does a lot of statistical analysis of matches and referees for the IRB. His presentation was about 'materiality' in refereeing and was designed to provoke thought and discussion with the aim of gaining consistency in referee's decisions. 'Materiality' basically means 'did the player's actions have an effect' and if so then the player is liable to sanction. Essentially, 'the times that you don't blow the whistle can sometimes make you a better referee'.

RWC referees are working within a framework comprising two elements:

• The IRB Charter—laws must be applied so as to ensure that the game is played according to the 'Principles of Rugby' which are 'through appropriate conduct and the right spirit, and through contest and continuity and fair play to score as many points as possible'; and

• The 'De Minimis'—a latin term, 'de minimis non curat lex', meaning 'the law does not concern itself with trivialities'.

So, as a referee we have to concern ourselves with the facts: was a law broken and was there an effect? This is the art of refereeing, because if we don't get this right there is the possibility of the game becoming unfair as you may penalise one thing and not the other.

An example would be when a player moves into an offside position and then immediately retreats and the referee does not penalise but plays on. In this instance the player broke the law but did not affect anyone, therefore you apply the theory of 'De Minimis'.

Did one side receive an unfair advantage or has one side been denied a fair advantage? The answer is no and the actions of the player is this case were immaterial to the game.

While this is easy in theory, its application relates to two types of 'immateriality'—factual and judgemental. Factual situations are those that are clear and obvious to all. However our discussion, through the use of sample video clips, concerned judgemental situations and was designed to make us take a breath and think about refereeing—to think before we blow the whistle so that we can effectively judge whether there has been an effect. The discussion was excellent.

Tim Gresson, RWC Tournament Head of Judiciary, and Darren Bailey, IRB Head of Legal, gave a talk on the tournament's judicial process. They emphasised that the referees and the judicial panel must be in sync for the integrity of the game. The most crucial element is that we are consistent in our rulings on foul play.

The last meeting for the day involved all the team coaches. Paddy O'Brien chaired the meeting with the assistance of the four selectors. The meeting aimed to clarify any issues about the law and its application as well as procedures for the tournament.

The IRB Chairman, Dr Syd Millar, addressed the meeting and pointed out that the tournament's success would result from all parties playing their part. There is a game 'aide memoire' that has been developed with the input of coaches, players, referees and administrators which explains the main interpretations of law and the spirit in which they will be applied.

Paddy explained that it is important that there are no sudden departures from that document as that is what the teams have been used to. While there was some clarification of the scrum call sequence that the referees had discussed the day before, the meeting was an opportunity to re-confirm the content of the 'aide memoire'.

Three major issues were highlighted: foul play, dissent and player clothing. These areas were highlighted to ensure that players are aware of the ramifications of their actions. It was an opportunity to remind participants of their responsibilities and hopefully this will mean that referees do not have to deal with these offences. However, if players do transgress then referees are expected to take the appropriate action. Paddy also explained that there would be no meetings between coaches and referees before games. The rationale behind this is that he wants us

At the 2007 Australian Super 14 Awards I won Referee of the Series.

Above: *Sin binning South African Springboks player Pedrie Wannenburg during the Tri-Nations Test at the Jade Stadium in Christchurch, 14 July 2007.*

Left: *My wife Fiona and I at Montpellier before refereeing my first match of the tournament, USA v Tonga.*

Bottom: *Team bonding in Tignes. From left to right: Malcolm Changleng (Scotland), Paul Marks (Australia), Craig Joubert (South Africa), Me and Simon McDowell (Ireland).*

Above: *Calling shot for goal in the USA v Tonga pool match at the Stade de le Mosson on September 12, 2007 in Montpellier, France.*

Left: *The opening ceremony of RWC 2007.*

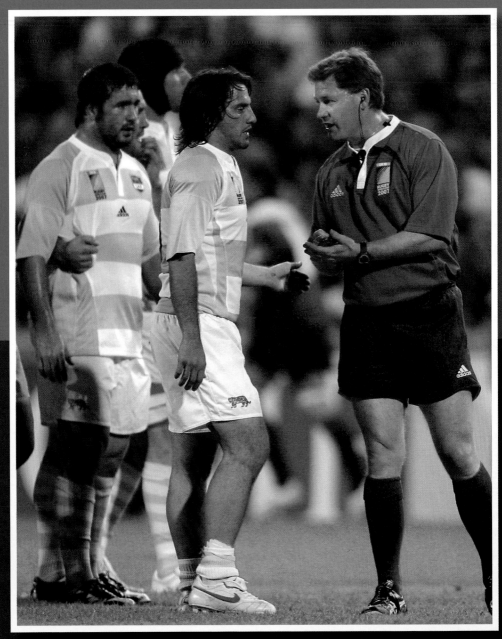

Above: *Speaking to Argentina's scrum-half and captain Gus Pichot during the Argentina v Namibia pool match on 22 September 2007.*

Top: *Awarding the match-winning try during the Pool B match between Wales and Fiji at the Stade de la Beaujoire on September 29, 2007 in Nantes, France.*

Right: *Awarding a penalty in the Wales v Fiji pool match in Nantes, on 29 September, 2007.*

Left: *Lunch in Andresý—what a magnificent rugby occasion.*

Centre: *Tossing the coin with the Welsh and Fiji captains, Gareth Thomas and Moses Raulini.*

Below: *Bernard Laporte, France's national team coach, at a training session at the Stade de France in Saint-Denis on 11 October 2007.*

to referee what is in front of us and not be swayed by any ideas that may be planted by coaches at those prematch meetings.

How the judicial system works at RWC 2007

The judicial system for RWC 2007 consists of a Citing Commissioner (CC), Judicial Officer (JO) and a three-person appeals committee that can be convened to hear the relevant matters.

In the first instance the CC will be sitting at a studio watching the match and he will have access to every conceivable camera angle that is available. They will then make notes in real time in relation to incidents that they see during the match as well as utilising the trigger of injured players whereby they will review the relevant footage to determine just how this fellow received the injury. They have a 48-hour window of time in which to complete this procedure and cite any relevant parties. The match officials fill in a report if we have either yellow or red carded a player and the CC will also contact us if they cite a person just to ensure whether we may or may not have seen the incident. The CC will use what they call 'the red card test' with their citings, which in layman's terms means that the act committed by that player if seen by a match official would have resulted in the player being sent from the field.

It is inevitable that there will be numerous citings and suspensions during this RWC. Our job as participants in the sport is to ensure that player safety is paramount—as with any decision there will be some who like it and some who don't. The only guaranteed way for a player to ensure they are not cited is to make sure they don't commit any acts of foul play.

Once the CC has cited the player he will appear at a hearing before the JO and the player will plead guilty or not guilty. If a guilty plea is entered then it is a matter of hearing any submissions from the player's counsel—then the JO will determine the sentence. If it is a not guilty plea then all the evidence will be heard, including that of the match officials if required in writing or in person, and the JO will then determine the case.

The appeals procedure is undertaken by a player if they feel they have been unfairly sentenced or there is other legal evidence pertaining to hearing and how it was conducted. That committee will then sit and hear the evidence from counsel and then make a determination on any of the matters that have been raised.

Wednesday 5 September: Our final group meeting before everyone began to disperse for the games. We discussed some logistical issues and formally wished Tony Spreadbury all the best for the opening match of the tournament.

I have to mentally prepare for three very different roles over the next three days. On Friday I will be touch judge for the opening match in Paris, on Saturday I will be television match official in Lens, and on Sunday in Paris my role will be No 4 offical—substitute controller/

reserve referee. I spent time reviewing some touch judge rulings and mentally visualising some positional play in order to ensure that I am in the correct place and frame of mind to make correct decisions. If you don't plan then you significantly increase the risk of failure and none of us want failure at this tournament.

It was then time to relax and our social committee, chaired by the one and only Tony Spreadbury, had organised an open-top bus tour around Paris. Off went the group of tourists and we had terrific time. Two hours of peace and quiet to just relax and enjoy the sights of this most magnificent city. My Australian colleague, Paul Marks was with the group and this is his first time in Paris as well as his first RWC. He was like a kid in a candy shop; he was absolutely mesmerised by the sights and the sounds of the city. It was a beautiful sunny afternoon and a balmy 20°C. It was wonderful to be able to see the gardens of Paris in full bloom as we usually travel here for matches in late autumn and winter. The town is splendidly decked out with Rugby World Cup signage and the Eiffel Tower has a massive RWC rugby ball suspended from the girders beneath the first level. Rugby fever has hit the town and we can't wait for the tournament to get under way.

Later in the afternoon we had a meeting with Rhys Jones, our video analyst, who demonstrated the computer system that captures all of the data from a match. It is called 'Fair Play' and was designed in Australia by Richard Hunter and his brother Jimmy. The operator watches the game and presses buttons to record the various events that occur when the game is being played. Each event has a video clip attached and at the end of the match you are able to retrieve every possible statistic you could ever want including the number of penalties, kicks in general play, tackles, passes and so on. It is an invaluable tool in helping us prepare and review games as you have all the information and clips at your fingertips.

Hugh Watkins from Wales, who is also part of the social committee, ran a 'pub quiz' in the evening. We are not sure whether he had had a premonition but he asked some questions about Luciano Pavarotti and some hours later we learnt the great man had passed away.

Touch judge preparation

Thursday 6 September: Today was very quiet with no official meetings, so everyone spent time getting ready for the games and travel coming up over the next few days. I went through my travel logistics and did some planning for my touch judging on Friday night. The roles of referee, touch judge and television match official (TMO) are obviously different and it is important that you change your mindset to be in sync with their specific requirements.

I caught up with Tony Spreadbury and Chris White (England) for a spot of lunch and also to check if there was anything Tony needed for the game the next day. We work a system where the referee of the day is essentially the 'team captain' and he makes the call for timings, dress code and any other necessary things prematch. As part of the referee team we are available to assist the referee at any time so that he doesn't have too much to worry about and can concentrate on on his preparation.

In the evening Monsieur Rene Horquet, a former French Test referee and current Treasurer of the French Federation de Rugby (FFR), hosted the entire referee team at a magnificent restaurant called Restaurant Le-Paris located at the Hotel Lutetia. Alan Lewis (Ireland) and Joel Jutge (France) arranged for us to sing to Rene and Monsieur Bernard Lappaset, the President of the FFR, when he dropped in later in the evening. The singing was a gesture of goodwill and thanks while also allowing us to embrace the culture of the country.

You can't overestimate how well these gestures are received and we wanted to show a mark of respect to the FFR for their organisation. We sang a famous French rugby song called 'Allez Le Stade' and Rene and Bernard were most appreciative of our gesture. It is another magnificent thing about this great game that it allows you to mix the rough and tumble of the game with a great tradition and history.

III.

The tournament begins:

The pool matches

THE RWC 2007 POOL DRAW

POOL A
South Africa
England
Tonga
Samoa
United States

POOL B
Australia
Fiji
Wales
Japan
Canada

POOL C
New Zealand
Scotland
Italy
Romania
Portugal

POOL D
Argentina
France
Ireland
Georgia
Namibia

Day 1: The opening game

Friday 7 September: For the opening game of Rugby World Cup 2007, Bryce Lawrence (New Zealand) and I will be touch judges. It is a great honour and a once in a lifetime opportunity. Refereeing history will be created tonight when Tony Spreadbury becomes the first Test match referee to have a father and son run touch for him during his career. Bryce's father, Keith Lawrence, former distinguished Test referee and now New Zealand Rugby Union Referee's Manager, ran touch for Tony in 1990 in an Australia v France match and now Bryce will be running touch for Tony 17 years later. We keep telling 'Spreaders' he is too old and this confirms it.

Bryce and I met to go over the various scenarios that could occur during the game. There has been a great deal of criticism of the standard of touch judging worldwide in the last 12 months and we wanted to make sure that we were prepared and would not let the team down. I spent the rest of the day taking it easy by reading and checking a few emails and we then had lunch as a group at about 3.30pm.

The match official team and the others going to the match met in the foyer of the hotel at 6.45pm and then set off in three cars to travel together to the Stade de France under police escort. With headlights and hazard lights on, the convoy moved into the street. Traffic in Paris is dodgy at the best of times with chaos and blaring horns a constant companion, however, when you add a police escort to that mix it is interesting to say the least. The drivers were told to keep close to each other and our driver took it to a new level—100km/h dodging and weaving through cars while being anywhere between a half and one metre behind the car in front.

Add to that a couple of police motorcycle riders who were hanging off their bikes kicking cars to get them to move over and you have a most enjoyable and funny 25-minute drive to the stadium. We had plenty of laughs and our driver enjoyed it when we started calling him 'Schumacher'. And once again, people say, 'Why would you want to be a referee?'. Eventually, I will think of an answer!

As we got near the stadium we felt the sense of occasion and atmosphere with hoards of supporters walking along in rugby jerseys with RWC banners everywhere.

At 7.30pm we went to the Argentinean changing room for the boot and gear inspection. When Tony, Bryce and I walked in the players were in a very relaxed mood. Bryce and I checked studs and padding and there were no problems.

In recent history player padding has started to resemble that of 'American football' and the IRB clearly stated this was not acceptable. I had a chat with Felipe Contepomi, the Argentine player who hugged me after their win in the 1999 RWC. I told him no cuddles tonight and he said, 'maybe if we win'. Their manner and body language showed they were up for the game and they had self-belief. As is customary we had a brief chat and wished them luck for the match.

We then checked the French dressing room. We checked the gear and again there were no problems. Bernard Laporte came straight over to have a chat and it was amicable with no hint of problems. I hadn't expected an awkward moment but it is always nice to get the next meeting over with when there has been some tension. We wished them the best of luck and then left. The two captains then met Tony for the toss, which France won.

The coin used for the toss is a commemorative coin that is usually on display in the New Zealand Rugby Museum in Palmerston North. This coin was used at the 1927 game played between New Zealand and England and has been used at the opening match of every Rugby World Cup. The William Webb Ellis RWC trophy was nearby and I took some time to have a close look at it. It was a really special moment and it re-confirmed the enormity of the occasion.

Tony, Bryce and I went out to have a look at the pitch. The surface was magnificent, the crowd so colourful and a there was a real buzz about the place. We had a photo taken and then walked around the ground to soak up the atmosphere and relax before kick off. The stadium was close to full with nearly 80,000 people. The noise was terrific.

We went back to our change room to put on our communications gear and warm up. I went back to the ground to sneak a look at the opening ceremony and managed to catch the awesome drum playing and also saw the fighter jets fly over trailing their red, white and blue smoke. I am really glad that I took the time out to enjoy the atmosphere.

We were all very relaxed and Spreaders was in fine form. At this time you are guided by the referee as to the mood of the room. If he is quiet and wants some time to reflect then you stay quiet, if they are talkative then you will chat a bit to help them ease the tension. Spreaders is very experienced and always composed and tonight was no different.

It was time to move out and we wished Spreaders good luck and moved into the tunnel where the teams lined up with us behind them. In 2003, the RWC organisers wanted referees to lead the teams out but we objected saying it is the players' game and they should be out first. The players moved out to a deafening roar. Loudest were the French supporters screaming *Allez les Bleus, allez les Bleus*.

I had a good look around to soak up the atmosphere. I really wanted to enjoy this moment. The singing of the French anthem in France is always magnificent but this time it was loud and passionate.

Jackets off, a shake of hands for the team of three and off to the touchline to get ready for the kick off. We were all very relaxed but you could now tell both teams were feeling the pressure and I saw a few of the French players taking a lot of deep breaths to help calm down. Along with commemorative coin there is also the whistle from the 1927 match and that has also been used to start each tournament. Tonight was no different as Tony blew that whistle and then very quickly put it in his pocket for safe-keeping.

The passion from both teams was evident from the start, however, so were the nerves, especially for France as they dropped the ball many times and missed opportunities to go wide and attack. The Argentinean team defended so well and that was basically the story of the match. It was not a classically entertaining match but it was great theatre as it was close, hard fought and passionate. Argentina held out to create a major upset and beat France.

They were so emotional and jubilant with all their staff running onto the field to embrace. Felipe Contepomi came up to say thank you and I very quickly told him 'no cuddles tonight'.

The Argentinean team played a basic match plan, designed to keep the pressure on France, by taking the opportunity to score points through penalty and field goals, as well as kicking tactically for field position and to make France run the ball back. As well as the kicks, it was important for Argentina to stay with their strength in the forwards and as such they mauled, used the 'pick and drive' and continually took the physical test to France. France was under massive pressure and this showed during the match, where they were tentative at times and kept a narrow focus.

In the dressing room after the match we congratulated Spreaders and talked about the last penalty goal attempt by Felipe Contepomi from Argentina. Time was up and the ball only needed to go over the posts or go dead and it was game over. We were all expecting him to belt it so hard that he would kick it into the forty-seventh row of seats but he missed the goal posts, giving France the opportunity to attack and perhaps win the match.

A number of people visited and congratulated Spreaders and the team and it was a great feeling to have been involved in this match. It will remain a treasured and special rugby moment.

DAY 1: 7 September 2007	
Pool A—Saint-Denis	
France	12
Argentina	17

Day 2: TMO for England v USA

Saturday 8 September: I was scheduled to be the television match official (TMO) in Lens for the England v USA game with Jonathan Kaplan (South Africa) as referee and Bryce Lawrence and Lyndon Bray from New Zealand as touch judges. We had Michel Lamoulie (France) travelling with us as the selector reviewing the game.

After getting to bed at 1am after the opening game it was a quick turnaround with the group leaving the hotel at 12.30pm with another police escort to the Gare de Nord railway station. All the boys are starting to feel a bit like royalty with police escorts everywhere. They certainly make short work of Parisian traffic. We had 'Schumacher' again and he tried to get even closer to the car in front than he did yesterday. I imagine the drivers are really enjoying the opportunity to travel at pace through their local streets and will have a great time telling war stories in the local café when the tournament is finished. At the station we were greeted by volunteers who make sure you get to the correct platform and train.

The ground at Lens was where I refereed the quarter-final playoff between Argentina and Ireland in RWC 1999 and received the 'little cuddle' from Felipe Contepomi. We arrived at Lens and—surprise, surprise—another police escort to the ground, albeit a very sedate one this time.

As television match official (TMO) you look at the replays to decide whether a try has been scored. It is part of our prematch process to meet the producer and inspect our equipment and location (sometimes inside the ground in a box or in the television production van). I started at 4pm just in case language was a barrier and also because we were using a system that was completely new to us. It was a smart move because security wouldn't let me in as my accreditation supposedly had the incorrect coding and then, after gaining a clearance, we met the technician who spoke no English and couldn't explain which buttons I needed to press to speak to the referee and producer. They were also meant to provide two stopwatches, as the TMO is the official timekeeper. My liaison man was unable to help as he also had limited English. No drama though, I had plenty of time so I just went down to the match commissioner and explained the situation. By 5.30pm everything was sorted out and I was ready to sit and wait for the game to start.

Kick off was at 6pm. For the first 15 minutes of the match I couldn't hear or speak to Jonathan due to technical difficulties. Luckily no decisions were required in that time. The match went well with the USA pushing England all the way.

I made one correct decision to award a try during the match. The process is straightforward: first, you stop the clock, listen to the question and repeat it back to the referee and then you have a look at the replays and make a decision. You then relay that call back to the referee and he will confirm your call and show the decision.

Later in the game Jonathan had a very strange moment as the England captain, Phil Vickery, had been replaced along with others and Jonathan was trying to find out who was the new captain. He then had Martin Corry and Lawrence Dallaglio, both former captains, standing in front of him and he asked the question of them as to who would be in charge. After embarrassed looks and a moment of silence Lawrence Dallaglio finally said 'I'll do it'.

In the change room I congratulated Jonathan and the boys on a great match. They spent some time filling out paperwork for the match commissioner about players that had been sin-binned. We caught the train back to Paris.

DAY 2: 8 September 2007	
Pool A—Lens	
England	28
USA	10
Pool B—Lyon	
Australia	91
Japan	3
Pool C—Marseilles	
New Zealand	76
Italy	14

Day 3: Three matches in three days

Sunday 9 September: I was pretty tired after a couple of long days and late nights with matches so I slept in. I was now onto my third match in three days and today I was No 4 official (substitute controller and reserve referee) for the South Africa v Samoa pool match at Parc de Princes in Paris. Paul Honnis (New Zealand) was the referee and Chris White (England) and Lyndon Bray (New Zealand) were touch judges.

I spent a good part of the morning relaxing and doing some

preparation for the game I'm refereeing on Wednesday. This was also good preparation for today—as reserve referee you have to plan as though you may actually get on the field at some stage and if you haven't done any preparation then your performance will reflect that. As a kid I think I attended scouts three times but I have borrowed their motto of 'be prepared'.

We left the hotel at 2pm for a 4pm kick off and guess who—yes 'Schumacher'–was again at the flight controls. Another crazy police escort as we flew through the streets of Paris. Sunday traffic was a little lighter but it was the same story with police, sirens, close driving and speed. I have been marvelling at one of the police motorcyclists who, while riding fast and moving traffic, has provided one of the most graceful sights you can see.

When moving the cars over he manages to roll his right arm from elbow to hand in a full circle with the grace and speed of a royal wave. It looks so magnificently elegant against the backdrop of the speeding motorcade chaos.

We arrived at the ground and proceeded to get changed. As a No 4 official you tend to leave the referee team alone to do their thing. I, of course, checked to see if Paul needed anything and then with the help of the local No 5 we sorted our paperwork. I had a walk on the field to look around and the atmosphere was terrific. There was a huge South African contingent and they were making plenty of noise. I caught up with Eddie Jones who was dressed in South African gear now that he is a consultant coach to the Springboks. Of course I gave him a bit of a ribbing about where his allegiances lay. We had a laugh but he did say he was really enjoying the challenge and had both taught and also learnt a great deal in his short time with the team. Jake White, the Springbok coach, also came over and we had a chat about all things rugby.

The match was a typically physical encounter with South Africa eventually outclassing the very willing Samoans. The crowd was terrific with the French contingent chanting 'Allez les Bleus' in support of the Samoans who also wear blue jerseys.

DAY 3: 9 September 2007

Pool A—Paris

South Africa	59
Samoa	7

Pool B—Nantes

Wales	42
Canada	17

Pool C—St-Etienne

Scotland	56
Portugal	10

Pool D—Bordeaux	
Ireland	32
Namibia	17

Day 4: Match plan for Montpellier

Monday 10 September: To prepare for the game I'm refereeing on Wednesday in Montpellier I went through my match notes and looked at some match footage on the 'fair play' system. I always prepare a 'match plan' that details the main areas that I need to concentrate on in a game. It helps me concentrate on the right issues and get into the correct frame of mind. As a referee you have to prepare physically, mentally and tactically for matches just as the teams do. It's also important to have a balance between preparation and relaxation because if you are too wound up that affects your performance.

Fiona arrived today and it was great to see her. I picked her up from Charles De Gaulle airport in the afternoon. After we checked her in to the hotel we headed into Paris. We went straight to a magnificent café called 'Angelina' that is located on the Rue de Rivoli opposite the park. We first discovered it on our honeymoon and it serves the best hot chocolate in Paris. We had a long walk in the park and onto Place de Concorde and then up the Champs Élysées before heading back to the hotel to pack for tomorrow.

Day 5: Suspensions

Tuesday 11 September: The journey south to Montpellier took about three and a half hours and the scenery was spectacular. The referee team assisting me with tomorrow's match is Craig Joubert (South Africa) and Christophe Berdos (France) as touch judges, Paul Honiss (New Zealand) as No 4 official, and Mark Lawrence (South Africa) as television match official (TMO).

We arrived at Montpellier in the afternoon to be greeted by blazing sunshine and 30°C temperatures. Montpellier is the home base for the Wallabies and I caught up with Scott Johnson, the Wallabies' assistant coach, before the team went to training.

Montpellier is a student town with a number of universities. The architecture is magnificent and the whole town was abuzz with people and RWC signage. The main square has a giant television screen set up so that people can watch the games and this square then leads off to the Opera House and numerous small alcoves and alleyways that house restaurants and shops. At the hotel I looked at some more clips of games and went over my notes to prepare for the game. At dinner the hot topic was the suspensions handed down by the judiciary. A US player, Paul Emerick, got five weeks for a dangerous tackle and England's Phil Vickery got two weeks for tripping. The judiciary was certainly taking no prisoners. Schalk Burger from South Africa was next in line that night but we would have to wait until the morning to find out.

Day 6: Referee, Tonga v USA

Wednesday 12 September. Finally, my first day of refereeing. The weather is hot with another 30°C day predicted. I had a meeting with the match officials team before leaving the hotel. As the referee you are captain of the team and these meetings are important because you can run through the requirements of each role and how you are going to work as a team. This includes touch judge positioning, what you would like them to call to you and what they should be looking at in certain areas.

We also found out that Schalk Burger had copped four weeks suspension and I pointed out that just because the judiciary had taken strong action we must not overreact, we should just do our job and look at what is clear and obvious in front of us. I was glad that the game was being played at 2pm, as I don't like sitting around and killing time for a night game. I felt really relaxed and was mentally prepared for what was shaping up as a 'RWC final' for both Tonga and USA as they appeared to be the weakest teams of the pool based on previous form.

We were taken to the ground at Montpellier with a police escort.

When we arrived I had a few butterflies in the stomach. That is always a good sign as it means I am focused and not too relaxed.

We met with the US team first. Their captain Mike Hercus is a Sydney boy who qualified for the USA as he was born there and holds dual citizenship. I talked to him about the need for players to stay onside during the game and for the tackler to move away so that the ball is available for quick play. I talked to the front row about the call sequence; I always let them know that I want them to tell me if they are not ready for engagement as safety is our primary concern. They appeared quite relaxed but Mike did say that they had a lot riding on this game.

We checked out the Tongan room and I had much the same discussion with their captain Nile Latu. I was given an official RWC coin to use for the toss. Tonga won the toss and elected to kick off; while the USA chose which way they would run.

Out on the ground for a warm up, the oppressive heat hit me straight away. I ran across the far side of the field and Fi came down to the fence to say hi and wish me luck. I completed my warm up and went back to the change room. A short time later we were waiting behind the players in the tunnel. When they entered the stadium the crowd cheered madly. The atmosphere was really special with people on their feet and plenty of flags and colour. The anthems started—I always make a point of watching a spectator and team member from each country when their national anthem is played. It emphasises the passion people have for the game and their team and I use that as a tool to refocus and make sure that I do my best. I took a moment to think of Dad and what we had discussed before his death earlier in the year. In his last days we had talked about rugby and I had said thank you to him for all his help and support and he told me that he just wanted me to do my best and make the family proud. It was certainly my intention to honour that dying wish.

The crowd of 25,000 was still when the Tongans gave a passionate performance of their prematch war dance. I did a final communications equipment check with the guys and started my heart rate monitor so I could check my levels after the match.

Tonga kicked off and the crowd was up as one. It was a free flowing match played in great spirit, eventually won by the Tongans 25–15. Both teams scored some great tries and it was close all the way through.

Both teams were passionate and had a great will to win and I thoroughly enjoyed the contest.

The US team had played only four days previously and the quick turnaround and the heat obviously had an effect as they seemed a little tentative at times. The more physical approach of the Tongans proved to be a deciding factor. The biggest problem that the US team faced was that their star centre, Paul Emereck, had been suspended for a dangerous tackle from the England game and that meant they were vulnerable in the midfield. Eventually this takes a toll mentally.

Our match official team worked really well together. Craig and Christophe reported one incident each and Mark had to make two

TMO decisions. The heat was amazing during the game and I had to drink plenty of fluid. My heart monitor showed that I averaged 136 bpm with a maximum of 177 bpm. I had an ice bath and shower to help cool down and flush out the lactic acid.

Fi and I met up with Ian Smith and Andrew Lees, two Sydney referees to reflect on the day. They had really enjoyed the match but not the sunburn!

DAY 6: 12 September 2007

Pool A—Montpellier	
USA	15
Tonga	25

Pool B—Toulouse	
Japan	31
Fiji	35

Pool C—Marseilles	
Italy	24
Romania	18

Day 7: Return to Paris

Thursday 13 September: Fiona and I left Montpellier on the 9.30am train to Paris. The journey took about three and a half hours and I spent some time writing a few notes for my review of the game. I will check them against the DVD footage. Unless it is absolutely necessary I won't do a proper review for at least two days as you need that time to remove yourself from the hype of the game so that you can look at it without the emotion. If you don't take that time then you tend to get yourself into a situation where you are protective and tend to try and justify things as opposed to listening to reasonable debate and that is not conducive to improvement of performance.

At this stage I was very happy overall and I really enjoyed the game and the passion of both teams. While there were no major refereeing mistakes I was also aware that I needed to look at a few minor positioning and communication issues. I am also not getting carried away with my performance as I have two games left in the pool rounds and each one is just as important in its own right. At this stage I was very happy with my performance and I really enjoyed the game and the passion of both teams.

Once back in Paris I picked up a DVD of the game and got some statistics about the match. I saw our physio Franck Tabanelli for a recovery massage. After training during the week and covering anywhere between eight and ten kilometres during a match it is really important to have massage to help the body recover.

In a former life Franck was a cyclist and represented France in the road race at the 1992 Barcelona Olympics. He told me that in one year with training, competition and recovery he would cycle approximately 35,000 kilometres. That is back and forth across Australia seven times!

In the afternoon Fiona and I took in the sights of the Opera House, Place de la Concorde, Champs Élysées and then had dinner at dusk with the Eiffel Tower as a backdrop.

Day 8: A big pool battle

Friday 14 September: The day started with a late breakfast where Fiona and I caught up with Tony Spreadbury (England) to have a chat before he headed off to Cardiff to be television match official (TMO) in the Australia v Wales match on Saturday and then referee the following day for Fiji v Canada.

Because I am not refereeing for another week, I can take some time out from the rugby and Fi and I can relax. We walked to Bastille and Notre Dame and then took a river cruise down the Seine to the Champs Élysées. The streets of Paris were a seething mass of humanity and it seemed as though every second person in the major tourist areas was either an English or South African supporter. The big pool match between South Africa and England is on at 9pm tonight and given the state of some of the supporters in the bars and brasseries, I wonder whether they will be awake or sober for the kick off.

We returned to the hotel in the late afternoon as we had to meet up with two mates from South Africa. Contrary to media reports in South Africa I do actually have friends in the country. My friends Jeff Andrews (originally from Scotland) and Mike Holsworth (originally from Wales) emigrated more than 20 years ago, and are now passionate South African supporters.

I introduced them to some of the other referees. I gave Jeff a number of match programs, some of which we had signed, as he is an avid collector. He was like a kid in a lolly shop and it was a good reminder that many rugby fans would give anything to be in my position where they can see, speak and interact with 'their' heroes, the players. We had a quick drink and a chat and they went off to the game full of hope for a South African win.

Fi and I watched the game on the television. South Africa were magnificent with pace, power and execution being the keys to their success. England just couldn't match it with them and South Africa was the deserved winner. The score was 36–0, a record defeat for England at a World Cup. It seems fairly obvious that the defeat will sting England and they will have two basic choices to make: do we wither and die or do we defend this cup with everything we have? The great sides will do the latter and it will be interesting to see how they will go. Having refereed them on many occasions I know they will choose to defend it with passion and I look forward to the pool contests.

DAY 8: 14 September 2007	
Pool A—Saint-Denis	
England	0
South Africa	36

Day 9: Preparing for the Islanders' match

Saturday 15 September: A return trip to Montpellier today as I will be the No 4 official in the Samoa v Tonga match on Sunday. Fi and I travelled with Jonathan Kaplan (South Africa), referee and Alan Lewis (Ireland), touch judge. Later that afternoon we met up with Bryce Lawrence (New Zealand), touch judge, and Lyndon Bray (New Zealand).

I watched the Australia v Wales match in the bar of the hotel. It was a very good game with Berrick Barnes playing a blinder as the last minute replacement for flyhalf Stephen Larkham. It was nice just to be able to sit down quietly and watch a game and enjoy the match and its place within the tournament.

The match officials group then met up in the early evening and shared a couple of glasses of wine and a lot of laughs. It was great for Fi to be there as the guys were so welcoming and made her feel a part of the team. We later found a small café and watched the Ireland v Georgia match. It was a close game won by Ireland 14–10. Ireland played poorly but the Georgians must be given full credit for their tenacity. They are big men who 'have a go'. In Georgia wrestling is the number one sport, so close physical combat is not a problem for them.

DAY 9: 15 September 2007	
Pool B—Cardiff	
Wales	20
Australia	32
Pool C—Lyon	
New Zealand	108
Portugal	13
Pool D—Bordeaux	
Ireland	14
Georgia	10

Day 10: No 4 official, Tonga v Samoa

Sunday 16 September: It was working up to another hot day in the south of France with a predicted temperature of 28–30°C. At least the match would be at 4pm rather than the 2pm start I had on Wednesday. There was massive anticipation from the locals and rugby fans worldwide as the Islander teams usually provide a very physical encounter and the spectators just love the 'big hits'.

We left at 2pm with another police escort. This one was probably the most sedate as there were not that many cars on the road. Ian Scotney, (Australia) had travelled down in the morning and joined us as the performance reviewer for the match. Once at the ground the match officials team went on the field to take a few photos to remember the occasion. As the No 4 official, I made sure that we had all the necessary paperwork, boards and drinks ready for the match officials. The No 4 and 5 referee ensure that substitutes are made at the appropriate stoppage and ensures the laws are adhered to in respect of the correct number and type of substitutions allowed. The No 4 and 5 are also responsible for ensuring the players warm up in their correct area and that the team medical people and runners also adhere to the rules.

When we lined up with the teams, we all wished Jonathan the best and walked onto the ground for the anthems. The atmosphere was terrific and the anthems were sung passionately. Everyone was relishing the prospect of the teams' prematch war dances.

The Tongans perform the *Sipitau* and the Samoans perform the *Siva Tau*. The custom for all the matches is that a ball boy or girl carries the match ball out with the referee and stands there during the anthems and then puts the ball on halfway and goes off the field. Jonathan motioned to the young fellow to put the ball down at the halfway as the Tongans were lining up for their dance.

The poor kid got confused, stopped, turned and faced the Tongans and stood there with the ball in his hands. The leader of the Tongans started the dance and moved around the kid while performing the ritual. The other 21 Tongans were advancing at the same time. He stood there like a rabbit caught in the headlights but he didn't flinch and that was pretty impressive. Once the war dance was finished he slowly put the ball down and we motioned for him to come over to us. He watched the Samoans from a safer distance.

The crowd gave both teams a massive ovation and the stage was set for a great game. Unfortunately, someone forgot to tell the teams. They both seemed to be tentative and for the first 60 minutes the normal flair and explosive nature of the games between the Islander nations was nowhere to be found.

It was close on penalties and then Tonga scored to take the lead and the crowd went wild. Tonga seemed to have the crowd's support as the underdog. It became very interesting as Samoa continually pressed the Tongan try line. Tonga had a player sent off and another player yellow carded through mad acts of foul play. Despite this the Tongans managed to hang on and win the game with only 13 players on the field for the last eight minutes.

When the final whistle blew, the crowd and Tongan players celebrated wildly. The look of delight, pride and passion on the Tongan players' faces was something to behold.

DAY 10: 16 September 2007	
Pool A—Montpellier	
Samoa	15
Tonga	19

Pool B—Cardiff	
Fiji	29
Canada	16

Pool D—Toulouse	
France	87
Namibia	10

Day 11: A day for the Aussies

Monday 17 September: The group returned from Montpellier in the early hours of this morning and it was around 1am before Fi and I got to bed. We were out of the hotel by 10am for a day trip with the other Aussies Paul Marks and Ian Scotney.

We had a great day with Marksy and Scotters. Scotters has been around the rugby world for a long time now and is well respected in his roles as a selector at Australian and provincial level as well as a performance reviewer and auditor at the international level. He was the chief organiser of this tour to Villers-Bretonneux to see the Australian War Memorial. This is a pilgrimage that I would recommend to any Australian in order to get an appreciation of just how brave and gallant our troops were and why we enjoy the freedoms we have today.

As we arrived at the little village of Villiers-Bretonneux it started to drizzle and the entire village had retired for lunch and would not be out again until at least 2pm. It was now 12.45pm so we trudged along a little further and found a 'Tabac' that was open. We ordered beers for the boys and hot chocolate for Fiona. We also managed to get potato chips and as far as we were concerned we had all the major food groups covered. We settled in to wait for the rain to stop so that we could head off to the War Memorial.

If you are not emotionally touched by this scene then you are not human. We walked through the graves to the monument that lists the names of almost 11,000 Australian diggers killed in action. You can walk up to the top of the monument and once there you look back over the gravestones and then gain a monumental perspective on how flat the terrain is and just how hard it would have been to find cover from fire and then to be so exposed as you attacked enemy positions. I just don't think words can describe my admiration and respect for all the soldiers but I am grateful that I could go again to pay my respects.

We went on to the Battle of the Somme Museum in a village called Albert. The museum is in the form of a tunnel that was converted into an air raid shelter in 1938. The tunnel is 250 metres long, 10 metres underground and has a series of 15 different alcoves with each depicting a scene from the era.

In the train back to Paris, we had time to reflect on what had been both an emotional and magnificent day.

Day 12: On my own

Tuesday 18 September: It was Fiona's last day and a chance for her to have a last look at Paris. We made our way to the Sacré Coeur in Montmarte and had a great time just strolling around and looking at the goods on sale and the people in the area and did the French thing by sitting at a little café, having a hot chocolate and just watching the world go by. Our liaison officer, former French Test referee Joel Dume, organised a car to take us to the airport. Fiona had a great time but missed the kids a lot. This break has been great for both of us as we got to spend some quality time together and saw a great many places and people. It will now be another five weeks until I see her again.

DAY 12: 18 September 2007	
Pool C—Edinburgh	
Scotland	42
Romania	0

Day 13: Reviewing my last match

Wednesday 19 September: In the morning I worked out my travel plans for the next week as I was refereeing at Marseilles and No 4 official at Toulouse. I also did some planning for my match on Saturday between Argentina and Namibia and had a look at some clips of both team's games on the 'fair play' system. I was looking at the scrums and lineouts to see if there were any patterns that have emerged in those games. You are not looking to pre-empt anything before you referee but it is important to do some homework and be prepared for any irregularities. With the aid of the 'fair play' system I could have a look at the lineouts of both teams and find out whether they are throwing to the front, middle or back on most occasions. This allows you to prepare your positioning. Again, the most important aspect is that you referee what is in front of you on the day and this information is just a help. I also picked up the report from Bob Francis about my first match, Tonga v USA. It was a good report and only highlighted some minor areas for improvement. The most important one was that I probably could have used a little more preventative management at the tackle.

In the afternoon I reviewed my game. My initial thoughts post-match had been the same as Bob's comments in the report. Now matter how much you prepare there is nothing like game time. I think everyone is in the same boat and you will always referee your second match better than the first as you are in a better groove.

I was pleased that the first one had gone well. That was now one tick in the box with two matches to go. But as I always say, 'You are only as good as your next game'. In reviewing my match I was looking at aspects of positioning to see whether I had missed things.

I also checked all the penalties to see whether I could make a better decision next time. As always you manage to find a few penalties that are not as clear-cut as you thought on the day. This is where Bob's view was correct that if I had managed a couple of situations better then I could have allowed play to continue rather than awarding a penalty. The decisions were 100 per cent correct but a better decision could have been made.

In the evening it was time to relax so I went to the movies with Dave Pearson (England) at a little village called Bercy just down the road from where we were staying. We found an English speaking cinema and saw *The Bourne Ultimatum*.

DAY 13: 19 September 2007	
Pool C—Paris	
Italy	31
Portugal	5

Day 14: Cheering the Japanese

Thursday 20 September Another quiet day before travelling tomorrow. I had breakfast with Chris White, Paul Marks, Tony Spreadbury and Dave Pearson. This was one of those moments where you relax from the busy schedule of the pool rounds. It helps achieve a balance between work and downtime.

When I arrived back I spent some more time with the 'fair play' system checking various aspects of Namibia's and Argentina's previous matches and some further analysis of my first game. The preparation has been good and I am feeling relaxed but I always find that I have a little bit of tension in the last couple of days before a match.

One of my good mates, David Kurk from England, was over for a couple of days and it was great to catch up with him. A whole group of us watched the Wales v Japan match on TV. The Japanese scored one of the tries of the tournament that went from one end of the field to the other. Rhys Jones and Hugh Watkins from Wales were there and I am not sure they were all that impressed with the remainder of the group leaping to their feet and yelling home the Japanese as they scored the try. It was a fast and furious game where tackling sometimes seemed optional. In the end, Wales managed to win it handsomely 72–18. I am refereeing Wales in a week's time when they play Fiji but I don't think this game will give me any great indicators for that match.

DAY 14: 20 September 2007	
Pool B—Cardiff	
Wales	72
Japan	18

Day 15: Marseilles and the 'pool of death'

Friday 21 September: It was time to travel to Marseilles so I could referee Argentina v Namibia on Saturday. The team for this trip was Kelvin Deaker (New Zealand) as the television match official (TMO), Simon McDowell (Ireland) and Carlo Damasco (Italy) as touch judges. Joel Jutge (France) would arrive later that evening and be the No 4 official.

One of the great aspects of this tournament has been the work done by the volunteers. We call them 'blue people' because they wear blue polo shirts. They escort us from the hotel to our point of departure, make sure all tickets are validated and put us on the correct plane or train. We are met at the other end by a similar group and escorted to our new hotel. This occurs no matter what the time of day or night. They have been wonderful hosts but there is a bit of overkill involved. Sometimes large numbers of blue people have met just one or two people. We now have a competition going to see who can garner the greatest entourage.

We have also taken to having a small bet to see how many will be there to greet us upon arrival. At Marseilles Deaks (Kelvin Deaker) was the closest with a guess of six blue people and two white people. The white people are the hostesses that wear a white dress and represent the TGV rail network who are a major sponsor of the tournament.

Marseilles has a magnificent harbour and our hotel has a view directly into the marina area where massive numbers of boats are moored.

After checking into the hotel we found a restaurant beside the marina that also had a television so we could watch the France v Ireland match. Simon was particularly interested as his nation was playing. Eventually, we managed to lift his spirits after Ireland were completely torn apart by the French, 25–3. This match was both teams' chance to attempt to get ahead of each other on the table so as to avoid missing out on the quarter-finals.

Argentina was the other top team and this pool was known as the 'pool of death' because one of these two top teams and Argentina could not fit into two available spaces. France were supported by a parochial home crowd and had the added pressure of having lost to Argentina in the opening match, however on this occasion they were far more relaxed and played a more expansive match whereas Ireland just seemed to be missing that something special and could not match the French.

The French led 12-3 at half time through penalty goals and came out in the second half and really clicked into gear and the Irish just couldn't match the pace or the physicality. France scored two wonderful tries in this half, one from a chipkick by Michelak back over the Irish pack on his right when he was facing left, which was scooped up by the winger who scored in the corner. The final result was 25–3 to France and they were deserved winners and now the pressure would be on for Argentina v Ireland later in the tournament.

It was a great night with great company and we shared a lot of stories and a lot of laughs.

DAY 15: 21 September 2007	
Pool D—Saint-Denis	
France	25
Ireland	3

Day 16: Referee, Argentina v Namibia

Saturday 22 September: I was really looking forward to this match as my games are spread out over the pool rounds, which is great for recovery and preparation but you also just want to get into it. The kick off was scheduled for 9pm.

After a late breakfast the afternoon flew by as we watched the South Africa v Tonga and England v Samoa matches at the hotel. South Africa v Tonga was a great match with South Africa finally getting home 30–25 after another spirited performance by the Tongan boys. These Pacific Nations sides along with Georgia were really mixing it up with the best.

The South Africans opted to start with some of the top line players on the bench and the Tongans took their opportunities and played well and were down 7–3 at half time.

They scored first after break and took the lead and that was when we saw the cavalry arrive in the form of John Smit, Victor Matfield, Juan Smith and Frans Steyn as very early substitutes. South Africa then took control and went out to a comfortable lead but Tonga came back with tries and in a thrilling finish South Africa had to defend with all of their might to scrape home 30–25.

Samoa had been built up as a team that was going to do well and unfortunately it was all downhill for them after their opening burst against South Africa. England controlled this match well and scored two tries in each half and just kept the scoreboard ticking over thus applying pressure to the Samoan boys who just could not match it with them. They played well in patches but ill discipline let them down on occasions and England punished them with points eventually winning the game 44–22.

This was my first time refereeing at Marseilles. The crowd outside the stadium was huge and the atmosphere was electric with a large number of Argentinean supporters already in attendance. The stadium holds about 60,000 and the massive stands on the three sides of the ground create an amphitheatre.

As we walked around the ground and took some photos we were greeted by a number of the Argentina players and the coaching staff.

Over the years the Argentineans have enjoyed their status as the 'little country' that does not get as good a deal as other nations. We referees are sometimes criticised for not being fair to the 'little country'. We take it in good humour most of the time and it is the basis of many jokes. I had told the boys that I would have a joke with the Argentina coach, Marcelo Lofreda.

We met on the field and I told him that tonight he was the 'big country'. He had a big laugh and immediately said 'No, Namibia is a close friend of South Africa so together they are a big country.' We headed back to the change room and started to get ready for the customary team checks, chat to the captains and front row, and then the coin toss. Both teams were very positive and said they were looking forward to playing an expansive game so they could entertain their supporters and themselves. The toss of the coin which was won by Argentina and their captain, Augustin Pichot, chose to kick off with the Namibia captain, Corne Powell, choosing which way to run. It was filmed for television and the backdrop was the Rugby World Cup trophy. Simon, Carlo and I decided that we wouldn't miss the opportunity and took our photos standing next to it.

With our warm up completed and communications gear set, it was time to leave the change room and go out to line up with the teams for the walk on ceremony. The crowd was really pumped up and the noise of the 55,000 in the stadium was incredible. The massive contingent of Argentinean supporters stood out in a sea of national flags and jerseys.

As the teams moved into position we wished each other good luck and did a final sound check to make sure the equipment was working well. The Namibians really had a go from the start. True to their word they had come to play and I think Argentina were a little taken aback as Namibia pressed forward with their attack. Namibia made an early break down the right and the Argentinean defender held onto the tackled player on the ground, which eventually resulted in Namibia getting a penalty. Suddenly Namibia was up 3-0 with the French members of the crowd going nuts and singing for the underdog. Initially Argentina played very loosely and dropped a lot of ball.

It was as though they thought they would score by just going through the motions. Argentina didn't help their cause with a lot of one out running with their players getting isolated and allowing the Namibians an opportunity to contest for possession. This is when you really go through the decision-making process. Did the tackler release? Are the arriving players on their feet and entering that area correctly? Has the tackled player released the ball?

The Argentinean boys were getting a little frustrated. I had also penalised the Namibians for being offside but Argentina had not been able to take advantage of this. They wanted four tries and a win to gain a maximum five points from the match but they were only getting penalty goals. I was being a lot more pro-active in my preventative management.

There are times when a player has offended and you must penalise immediately. Other times you can get in early and ask a player to move away or ask them to move onside to keep things flowing. Using downtime, when there is an injury break for example, is also important. I was talking to both teams, Namibia had given away a few penalties and I was asking for co-operation from Corne and his team. Gus Pichot, the Argentinean captain, was also frustrated and I had to keep him calm. He has a history of having a chat and you just have to put him in his place at times. I explained to him that his boys were getting isolated and that it was then a fair contest for the ball—he should just take a breath and relax.

Argentina eventually scored their first try and Gus questioned me again about the Namibian team slowing down the ball. I let it go and after Felipe Contepomi had kicked the goal I had a chat with him and asked him to have a chat to Gus to settle him down. I told him that I had played advantage and they had then scored the try. I was managing the situation and it was in hand. He went straight down and relayed the message and Gus looked up with a big smile and two thumbs up. In these situations you are trying to put out a fire before it becomes a problem. Sometimes you need to be a bit more creative in the management and the use of another senior player can be helpful.

Argentina finally found their rhythm and scored two more tries before half time. I had to go to Deaks as the television match official (TMO) on two occasions and they were both tough calls.

The Namibians tried their hardest and could be justifiably proud of their wholehearted effort. However the difference in class showed in the second half with the Argentineans running in another six tries to win the match 63–3. They attacked with great flair and some of the tries were just a pleasure to watch. They mixed great skill with great strength and unfortunately for Namibia they just weren't able to cope. Even though it was a lopsided scoreline it was a great match played in great spirit and I really enjoyed the entire experience. I was really pleased with the match official teamwork as Carlo and Simon were great on touch as was Deaks in the TMO box.

DAY 16: 22 September 2007

Pool A—Lens

South Africa	30
Tonga	25

Pool A—Nantes

England	44
Samoa	22

Pool D—Marseilles

Argentina	63
Namibia	3

Day 17: Questions for myself

Sunday 23 September: This morning was the hardest and most emotional time away from home as Fi rang and I talked to her and the kids. When I spoke to Michael he started crying and told me how much he missed me and wanted me to come home so I could be with them all and watch him play t-ball. This is the hardest thing we have to deal with in this job. Press reports and people's opinions are nothing compared to your family. Trying to console your six-year-old son on the phone when you are on the other side of the world is just so hard and I know I have another month still to go. I cried when I put the phone down. We all go through it and you just have to get on with it and do your best.

Later on we set off on the four and a half hour train trip to Toulouse. We were all so tired from the various activities and travel over the past weeks that we caught up on some sleep. I made a few notes about the previous night's match. All in all I was really happy with the match and the score line certainly didn't indicate the amount of refereeing I actually had to do for such a lopsided encounter.

My focus was on how I could do things a little better for the next game. I had awarded a penalty try to Argentina because the Namibian scrum disengaged as Argentina was going for a pushover try from five metres out. The question was—should I have waited just a few more seconds for Argentina to score and be incorrect at law or stay within the law and give the penalty try? You review these matters as you want to work out what the best decision would be. For me it was all about, 'Do I actually want to be bringing any unnecessary attention to myself?'

DAY 17: 23 September 2007	
Pool B—Montpellier	
Australia	55
Fiji	12

Pool C—Edinburgh	
Scotland	0
New Zealand	40

Day 18: Time out in Toulouse

Monday 24 September: Toulouse is a lovely little city and is home to a very large university and one of the best-supported rugby teams in the country. It is definitely French rugby heartland. Simon McDowell (Ireland) tells me that refereeing European Cup matches at the stadium is something quite loud and special. It was our intention to just have a complete break from all things rugby for the next two days until match time.

Unfortunately, I missed an excursion to a nearby village to look at the *pâté de foie gras* market. I woke with a massive headache and some minor flu symptoms so I took a couple of paracetamol and went back to bed.

In the afternoon we visited a wine co-operative in the town of Fronton. This wine label is one of the most famous in France and is known worldwide as a premium product. The co-operative made an extraordinary 95 million litres of wine last year. We also visited a vineyard to watch the grapes being harvested by machine.

Day 19: No 4 official, Portugal v Romania

Tuesday 25 September: Toulouse has a very large Portuguese population and I knew they would be out in force tonight to support their team in the Portugal v Romania match. This match would be both team's RWC final. They had both lost all their other matches and tonight would allow one team to go home having had a win at the tournament.

The match was due to kick off at 8pm so we went on an Airbus factory tour in the morning so we could see the new A380 planes and the retired Concorde. I ran into friends from Sydney, Tammy and Maurice Doria and their boys Hayden and Antony, who were also doing the tour. I also bumped into another fellow I had met through his company's sponsorship of the referees in Sydney. There certainly are plenty of rugby people travelling the world to this great festival.

Tonight I was No 4 official with Paul Honiss (New Zealand) as referee, Simon McDowell (Ireland) and Carlo Damasco (Italy) as touch judges, and Kelvin Deaker (New Zealand) as the television match official

(TMO). We had another police escort to the ground and the vibe at the stadium was terrific with Portuguese and Romanian supporters turning up in great numbers. There were also many French rugby supporters. Just like in Australia in 2003, the local people have really embraced the tournament and given it great support—it has become an international occasion.

The quality of the stadiums around France has been fantastic. The RWC has used a lot of the soccer grounds that were upgraded for the Soccer World Cup in 1998. They allow the crowds to be close to the action and the organisers have also had bands playing trumpets inside the ground to get the crowds going. This stadium had a capacity of 38,000 and the crowd for tonight's game was nearly 36,000 and they generated a huge amount of noise.

As usual, we all walked out behind the teams and stood for the national anthems. Earlier in the evening I caught up with Adam Leach, an Australian coach, who was doing some technical coaching work with the Portuguese team. He told me how their coach had spoken to the players about what an occasion this was for Portuguese rugby and the pride he had in his team.

Adam said that a number of the players could not move from their seats for a long time and that he had thought it probably one of the best and most emotional prematch speeches he had ever heard. I stood next to the Portuguese team and I was just blown away at just how forcefully and emotionally they sang their national anthem. This was a great rugby moment and the crowd gave them a huge ovation.

The game itself was a willing contest with Romania clearly the stronger of the two sides. Portugal played with such courage and determination and although they lost 14–10 they could be justifiably proud of their effort. There has been huge debate during the tournament in relation to whether these second tier sides should be playing against the top nations and calls have been made for the RWC 2011 to have only 16 teams. I can see merit in both arguments but at this tournament some of these 'lesser' teams have stepped up and provided some stiff competition and some really great moments with their passion and willingness to just have a go. The crowds and rugby public have really appreciated it.

After the match we stayed on the field while the Portuguese team received their RWC participation medals. It took some time to get the team in order as both teams were doing a lap of honour to the delight of the crowd.

Our liaison man, Franck, told us to hang around as something special was going to happen after the presentation. As the team stood in line a picture of one of the players and his girlfriend flashed onto the screen with the words 'will you marry me?' This fellow's girlfriend had arranged this and the players were also in on it as they suddenly put on t-shirts printed with the photo of the couple. Of course the guy said yes.

With this game over I could now allow my mind to start thinking about my next refereeing appointment—Wales v Fiji on Saturday in Nantes. This was going to be a knockout game as the winner would qualify second in the pool and make the quarter-finals and the loser was finished.

DAY 19: 25 September 2007	
Pool B—Bordeaux	
Canada	12
Japan	12

Pool C—Toulouse	
Romania	14
Portugal	10

Day 20: Return to Paris

Wednesday 26 September: The trip back to Paris took five hours and we all had a chance to catch up on some sleep and have a chat about the tournament. Jonathan Kaplan refereed the Japan v Canada match last night. There had been a problem because no-one stopped the stadium clock during injury time. The clock was showing 84 minutes when Japan scored and tied the match 14–14. The television match official (TMO) and referee were in complete control and knew time was correct at 80 minutes but the time on the scoreboard obviously caused a huge amount of concern for the Canadian players and fans. The IRB has scheduled a meeting to sort something out with the host authorities and will also put out a press release confirming the referee and TMO were correct. These are the sorts of things that create controversies for match officials and just shouldn't happen in the first place. Another point of discussion was the complaint about the standard of the television coverage. Many viewers and some television companies have been criticising the vision provided by the host broadcaster saying that it has either been too far away or too close and that replays were often poor or non-existent. It is hard to argue against that view.

I had also started to think about my match on Saturday and made some notes. To be ready for this game I need to be focused and relaxed and make sure that my preparation is similar to the other games, as they had gone really well.

DAY 20: 26 September 2007

Pool A—St-Etienne

Samoa	25
USA	21

Pool D—Lens

Georgia	30
Namibia	0

Day 21: Fair play and Euro Disney

Thursday 27 September: I woke at 6am and did a training session to prepare for my upcoming game, even though a trip to Euro Disney had been arranged for us today. It was a really relaxing time, even if you do include the dizziness after riding 'Space Mountain'. It was once again a good chance to catch up with Chris White and Tony Spreadbury (England) who are really good mates. It was also a chance to check on 'Whitey', in the flesh, after his 'collision' with the players during last Friday's Ireland v France game.

I ran into some teachers and girls from a school in Tamworth who were in France for the RWC and other cultural wonders. They were so excited about their trip, Euro Disney and the rugby. I bought a couple of gifts and took a load of photos for my kids.

It was then time to head back to do a bit more work for the game. I always manage to do some preparation after wandering around, as your mind during downtime will suddenly think about some aspect of the match. I looked at the 'fair play' system to assess where both teams may throw the ball in the lineouts, and also checked aspects of their scrummaging. I made some notes about my philosophical approach to the match. The main thing for me was to ensure that I referee what is in front of me and not concern myself with what is at stake for the teams. My aim is to ensure there is a fair contest and then let the players work out how even that contest is.

Day 22: Psyching up for Nantes

Friday 28 September: I am now one day away from refereeing my last match in the pool rounds—Wales v Fiji in Nantes. I am really looking forward to the game as it will be like a quarter-final as the tournament is all over for the loser. Our team for this game is Kelvin Deaker (New Zealand) and Simon McDowell (Ireland) as touch judges with Carlo Damasco (Italy) as the TMO. Megan Deaker was also travelling with us again and we have had a sensational time as a tour group.

We have enjoyed each other's company and been welcomed everywhere we have visited by local people who have shown great hospitality and this has been a great factor in helping me achieve the balance between thinking about rugby and getting away from it all.

We were met by the blue people and transferred to Montparnasse Station for the two hour journey to Nantes. Simon can speak a reasonable amount of French so he helped me find a hairdresser so I could get a haircut. His translation skills ensured I ended up with something close to normal. I had a wander around the town before dinner and had more of a think about the match, my philosophy and processes. That all sounds a bit heavy and deep but in fact it is merely taking the opportunity to put your mind at ease and make sure you have covered all the bases which is the only way to ensure you give yourself a chance at performing your best. I was feeling a little nervous, which is a good sign, but I certainly wasn't allowing those nerves to take over.

DAY 22: 28 September 2007	
Pool A—Paris	
England	36
Tonga	20

Day 23: Referee, Wales v Fiji: 'What a game'

Saturday 29 September: I had a terrible night's sleep. I didn't dream or wake up thinking about the game; I just couldn't get to sleep. After such a bad start there was no way I would have thought in a million years that today would involve the greatest game of rugby I have ever had the pleasure to be involved in.

Today would be the last match for Kelvin, Simon and Carlo as the group of thirteen touch judges would be heading home on Tuesday. I had a chat with Carlo about our TMO/referee relationship for the day. This was especially important as English is Carlo's second language and his job as television match official (TMO) could be a deciding factor. We needed to ensure we were prepared and that nothing would be lost in translation. This would be Carlo's biggest match as TMO and we joked with him that he was the man under pressure—his decisions may send a team home.

I walked into town to meet up with Geoff Acton, one of my great mates and fellow Australian Panel Referee, who was in Paris with his family on a holiday and had come down especially to watch the match. We watched the first half of New Zealand v Romania on the big screen in the town square.

At 2.45pm Kelvin, Simon and I had a meeting about our teamwork for the match. The support that the team of three gives to each other is crucial and as a referee you need these guys to be in tune with the match and with you to assist you to make the best decisions. They need to be your eyes and ears for the areas that you just cannot physically cover.

My cousin Rob and his wife Lynne had come from London to watch the match. Having been away from home for such a long time it was a great feeling to have family around and this really added to the occasion and at the same time helped me relax and focus. I admit I was a little nervous, but probably more excited than anything.

Nantes Stadium is a fantastic venue. The crowd is close to the field and the playing surface is like a bowling green. The crowd was already there in numbers. I walked onto the field to have a good look around and already there was a feeling of anticipation and excitement. I just soaked it all up. Alain Rolland (Ireland) was our No 4 and Stephen Hilditch (Ireland), the selector on duty, were at the ground already, having travelled from Paris that morning.

I changed into my referee gear before meeting the teams for a chat and gear inspection. On Friday Syd Millar, IRB Chairman, had sent out a text to all the referees and selectors explaining that scrum feeds were a major issue and a blight on the tournament and this area would be taken into account when referee selections were made for future matches. I checked that the halfbacks had been made aware of the IRB statement in relation to putting the ball straight into the scrum and then reinforced it.

It was a special day for the Welsh captain, Gareth Thomas, who would play his one hundredth Test match. He would be the first ever player from Wales to do so. I congratulated him and then went out to toss the coin. The crowd had built to nearly full capacity and the singing and atmosphere were just electric. As I did my warm up I looked at supporters of both teams and I could read the anticipation and hope in their faces.

We lined up in the tunnel and walked out with the players. It was an amazing sight and cacophony of sound—the crowd just went nuts. I always take out my earpiece so I can get the full sound and the noise was deafening. The anthems were sung intensely by both teams. The Fijians then performed an inspirational *cibi*, their tribal war dance. The crowd was now whipped into a frenzy.

I blew time on and we were under way. The first few minutes of play were patterned, well drilled and Wales' early attack was an indication of the brilliance and tension that would be the hallmark of this match. Wales began to run and create some space and I had to penalise Fiji for going off their feet and stopping the Welsh attack. I spoke with Moses

Raulini, the captain, and reminded him that his players needed to be positive. He spoke to his players and many times during the match he was yelling to them to stay on their feet and to keep the discipline.

Wales took an early lead from a penalty goal. The Fijians then put on a show of raw power and precision over a ten-minute period that only the Islander teams are capable of. They ran with great pace, created space with angles and deft passes and scored three of the best tries you would ever see in a game of rugby. They absolutely tore the heart out of the Welsh team and their supporters. Fiji were now leading 25–3.

The shell-shocked Welsh managed to come back to score a pushover try as their scrum was just so powerful and annihilated the Fijian pack. They had now closed the score to 25–10. The Fijians committed two dangerous tackles, one high and one late, and I told Moses that the next indiscretion would see one of their players going to the sin bin. A short while later one of the Fijian players lifted a knee when a Welsh player entered a maul and Kelvin reported it to me. The act itself was innocuous but as this was now the third case I followed through on my word and duly sent the player to the bin. James Hook missed the conversion from in front and Fiji went into half time leading 25-10.

During the half-time break we switched our communications gear off so we could chat about how things were going and discuss any areas of concern. The consensus was that we were going to have a hell of a game in the second half as Wales had to play and score points.

When we came back out the roar of the crowd was louder than at the opening of the match. Fiji kicked off and Wales came out with determination to play and to win. Both teams threw the ball around and we went from side to side and end to end with some great movements from both teams.

This half it was Wales' turn to up the ante and they scored four brilliant tries. Shane Williams, the Welsh winger, scored an absolutely magnificent solo try with a theatrical dive at the end that was worth 9.5. He ran and beat players with pace and step and it was a joy to watch. The Welsh were on fire and were staging a comeback. It was just incredible being in amongst it, let alone imagining how it was as a spectator. The Welsh then took the lead with their third converted try. It was now 29–25 and the stadium was erupting.

The physicality of the contest was huge, with the Fijians making some massive tackles and imposing themselves in the midfield. The game continued to flow from end to end and about three minutes later the Fijians kicked a penalty goal to make it 29-28. Six minutes later they kicked another one to go back into the lead 31-29. The noise of the crowd was intense with the possibility that Fiji may just win the match. For me, it was a matter of staying calm and not getting caught up in the emotion. That would seriously effect the decision making and neither team needed a problem like that.

The Fijians made a break down the right-hand side and their winger Delasau dived for the corner. At the same time he was tackled into touch by Gareth Thomas. I asked my Italian mate Carlo to rule whether a try had been scored and all his worst nightmares descended upon him. A crucial match altering decision and it was so, so close. He correctly ruled no try.

The Fijians kept throwing the ball around and Martyn Williams intercepted and started to run nearly the length of the field to score. I knew he was clear and my only concern was to make sure I would get there with him when he scored—at least inside the 22m area. No referee wants to join the '22 metre Club' which is when you are not in the 22 metre area at the time a try is scored. I made it and was well inside by 10 metres when he touched down. The Welsh supporters went ballistic. Wales had now regained the lead and the score was 34–31. What a contest! I kept telling myself to keep concentrating and finish the job.

The noise and atmosphere was now unbelievable. Fiji kept pressing in attack and were not going to give up. They mounted a late attack with 'pick and drive' close to the line and when they finally went over the noise was deafening. The player with the ball landed amongst the bodies and I was unsure whether he had clearly grounded it. I spoke to Kelvin and he said to go up to the TMO.

I asked Carlo, 'Can you tell me if a try has been scored?' This was a massive decision as it would put Fiji into the lead. The tension was huge for the players and I imagine the pure theatre was just incredible for those at the ground and watching on the television.

Carlo came back to me and confirmed it was a try. When I awarded it the stadium erupted. Nicky Little then kicked the goal and it was 38–34. The Fijians were in with a chance of doing what many thought impossible. Fiji eventually gave away a penalty inside their own half and as time was up on the clock Wales called for a scrum in order to create more space in the field to attack from. They kept the ball alive and went from side to side and then one of their players got isolated and the ball was trapped. I blew the whistle to stop the players and then blew it again to signal the end of the match. The crowd erupted and the Fijian players were ecstatic. The Welsh were gutted.

My touch judge Simon was the closest to me and we shook hands. We still couldn't quite believe what we had just been involved in. I am at a loss for the right words to describe just how it felt. I was mentally exhausted as the pace of the game and the decision-making was incredible. We went to the change room and just sat down to try and soak it all in and relax for five minutes before we had to go back out for the medal ceremony for the Welsh.

I thanked Simon and Kelvin for a great job and I was just so happy that they got to finish the tournament on such a high. They had been such great support and had put aside any disappointment they may have felt at not being selected as referees to be just magnificent team men.

We made our way back on to the ground and it was an incredible sight. The Fijians were doing a lap of honour with the whole crowd responding. The Welsh players were standing around looking totally despondent.

We moved well away to the side and I looked around to savour the moment.

The Welsh players received their medals and in a great gesture Gareth Thomas saw us and went out of his way to come all the way over to say thank you and well done. It was a great gesture and my respect for him grew. He did not have to come over at all given the circumstances of his despondency but full credit to him.

Carlo Damasco had come down from the TMO box and he was just a sight to behold, with his tie around his chest, top button undone, shirt hanging out at the front and his suit nearly falling off his shoulder. He looked a mentally tortured dishevelled mess. He had to make two of the toughest TMO decisions anyone could be asked to, and he had got them both 100 per cent correct. We congratulated him on a job well done and he said that he would probably like to run touch more than be TMO.

It was an amazing day and one I will never forget. It was a great honour and privilege to be involved with such a game where the players gave so much for their countries. I suppose this is the time when sport can be both sweet and sour but in time all the participants will reflect on what a magnificent and historic occasion it was.

DAY 23: 29 September 2007

Pool B—Bordeaux	
Australia	37
Canada	6

Pool B—Nantes	
Wales	34
Fiji	38

Pool C—Toulouse	
New Zealand	85
Romania	8

Pool C—St-Etienne	
Scotland	18
Italy	16

Day 24: TMO, Ireland v Argentina

Sunday 30 September. Today I was television match official (TMO) for another knockout game between Ireland and Argentina at the Parc de Princes in Paris. I had a chat with Stephen Hilditch on the train and he was happy with my performance in yesterday's match and said he was delighted he had been present at one of the greatest RWC games ever played. The best thing about a game like that is that the match official team had not been involved in contentious decisions that had influenced the game. It had been a great day and many players and referees go through a career and don't even get close to something like it. I was No 4 when Andre Watson refereed the thriller between Australia and New Zealand in Sydney in 2000 when Jonah Lomu scored right at the end to win the game and that was brilliant. Having now been in the middle of one it was just a wonderful feeling.

Back in Paris it was time to pay attention to today's match. It was really important that I now changed my focus from the high of refereeing yesterday's game, to the job at hand. I was still euphoric about the Wales v Fiji game, but as referees we must live in the here and now. While it had been a taxing match physically, I was fully refreshed and ready to focus on Ireland and Argentina. Paul Honiss was refereeing and he would equal the legendary Derek Bevan of Wales' world record of 44 Test matches.

We had a police escort and Paul filmed the entire thing. The police had been told we would be filming so they put on a show with wheel stands, immaculate arm signals and riding manoeuvres that were amazing.

I went into the change room with the guys and then out onto the field to have a look around. Once again the atmosphere was electric. The Argentine and Irish supporters were singing and enjoying themselves and obviously looking forward to a win by their team. Unfortunately there would be only one winner and someone would be going home. I went up to check that all the TMO gear was in place and working and saw the producer to confirm a time to check audio and video transmissions with him.

Ireland needed to win this game to stay in touch for at least second place in Pool D. They certainly played a lot better than they had in previous matches but Argentina were able to keep pressuring them into mistakes and at the same time keep the scoreboard ticking over. They scored two tries to one in the first half and once again mixed up limited backline movements with kicks for field position and 'pick and drive'.

The crowd was a great factor in the game with loud support for both teams. Argentina took an 18-10 lead into half time.

The second half was even more intense, with Ireland scoring a try from a brilliantly worked backline move from lineout possession that narrowed the margin. Argentina were then able to get into a field position that allowed their flyhalf to kick three penalty goals and a drop goal—adding points and pressure.

The Argentineans defended well and restricted Ireland to that try for their only points in the second half. No matter what Ireland did in the match the Argentineans had the answer. Whether it was a driving maul, passing movement, or tactical kick, Ireland just could not find a way through and Argentina were deserved winners of the match 30-15. They would now live on in the tournament. I wasn't required to make any decisions as a TMO in this game and that was fine.

It was incredible to see that two of the 'Six Nations' teams were gone in a matter of two days. The Argentinean team and supporters were going mad and all the talk around the stadium from players, supporters and administrators related to how these two 'minnows', Fiji and Argentina, had inflicted a massive blow to the order of world rugby. As Argentina had won their pool it set up a New Zealand v France quarter-final in Cardiff.

DAY 24: 30 September 2007	
Pool A—Montpellier	
South Africa	64
USA	15
Pool D—Marseilles	
France	64
Georgia	7
Pool D—Paris	
Ireland	15
Argentina	30

IV.

The Quarter-finals

Day 25: Quarter-final decisions

Monday 1 October: It was a strange feeling today with the anticipation of selection for the quarter-final referees and the touch judges leaving. Tonight was our last evening together as a full group. We had a 'court session' planned as well as farewell drinks with the hotel staff and then a dinner paid for by Mike Miller, CEO of the IRB.

The selectors were meeting for most of the day. It was a full house, with David Pickering (Chairman), Kevin Bowring, Stephen Hilditch, Michel Lamoulie, Tappe Henning, Bob Francis and Paddy O'Brien all locked in a room discussing the remaining RWC matches and the Six Nations appointments.

We all met to hear the results of their deliberations at 5pm. In attendance were only the selection panel and the referees. David Pickering began by explaining that making the selections had been hard work and that nothing further should be read into the appointments. They would make the selections for the semi-finals the following Monday.

There was an air of suspense in the room and for everyone's well being they got on with the job straightaway and announced the referees for the quarter-finals. It was Alain Rolland (Ireland) for Australia v England, Wayne Barnes (England) for New Zealand v France, Alan Lewis (Ireland) for South Africa v Fiji and Joel Jutge (France) for Argentina v Scotland. There was a great round of applause for the guys and congratulations all round. I was selected as the No 4 for New Zealand v France in Cardiff and then touch judge for Argentina v Scotland the next day. This would mean travelling to Cardiff on Friday and then a lightning trip back to Paris on Sunday morning for the game in the evening. I am really looking forward to these matches—to be involved in any capacity is great. Of course, I am also looking forward to next Monday to see what happens.

It was time to get into our 'court session', when the match officials hold a mock court session where punishments are dished out to various offenders. The money collected is donated to charity.

The prosecutors were Mr Wayne Barnes, fairly apt as he is a barrister, and Mr Hugh Watkins, just because he is a great bloke and a very funny Welshman. The presiding judge was none other than His Honour Anthony Spreadbury (England). The door was locked and any latecomers were fined which was unfortunate for Alan Lewis and Joel Dume. Now court sessions being as they are, there is no justice and fair play is out the window. His Honour fined his English mates except for Mr Barnes whose fine was doubled. I was charged with shaking hands with Bernard Laporte (French coach) in the French changing room prior to the opening RWC game.

It was really well scripted and very funny with plenty of fines resulting from somewhat embellished stories. Nobody was spared. Jonathan Kaplan's was probably the funniest as he was charged with 'Endangering the Health of a Minor and Causing Permanent Psychological Harm to that Same Said Minor'. There was video footage to go with it and we literally had tears rolling down our cheeks. Jonathan had been the referee for Samoa v Tonga and had told the ball boy to put the ball on the halfway line. This was lost in translation and the poor kid just stood there facing the Tongans and remained stock still with ball in hand as they proceeded to go through their tribal dance around him. The poor kid looked petrified and of course JK pleaded guilty.

We had drinks with the hotel staff so they could wish the touch judges bon voyage. Then it was off to a little restaurant around the corner owned by a former player. They closed the restaurant to the public, which was fantastic as we could just relax and have a great time. There were many speeches and presentations and it was a wonderful night that allowed the team to say thank you to the IRB for hosting the dinner and formally thank all those people who have helped to make this one of the best refereeing groups at any RWC.

Mike Miller, CEO of the IRB and RWC, presented us with participation medals and David Pickering thanked us for the efforts of the group so far. He also reminded us that a new phase had started and that we must improve on the high standards that had been already set. As the night went on and the consumption of varied beverages continued, the singing began and soon the anthems of each country represented were in full flight as well as many rugby songs and great revelry into the evening. It was just a brilliant time and something that I will cherish as a great memory from what has been a wonderful tournament. One of the greatest highlights for me was to listen to Nigel Owens (Wales) singing as he has the most magnificent voice and dabbles as an entertainer part-time. If you ever get the chance to see and hear him, don't miss it.

Day 26: Preparing for a new tournament

Tuesday 2 October: The touch judges have left and we are down to 12 referees to fulfill all the roles of referee, touch judge, TMO and No 4 and 5 officials.

It is around this time in the tournament that you start hearing stories about long lost aunties, friends of friends, old neighbours and the like who suddenly re-appear in your life as your best mate to see 'how you are' and then want to check whether you can possibly get them a spare ticket. We could make a fortune, but we had to sign a contract prior to the tournament that prevents us from doing just that. Federico Cuesta (Argentina) was staying on for another week, having finished his duties as a touch judge. I was more than happy to help his family out with my tickets for the Argentina v Scotland match.

After lunch we had a meeting with the referees and selectors about the quarter-finals and beyond. It was an opportunity for Paddy to re-focus the group. The first point was to review the processes for extra time and the kicking competition if the matches are tied at full-time. For quarter-final matches, semi-final matches, the bronze final and the final, if teams are tied at full-time, then a multi-step process determines the winner. First, there is 20 minutes of extra-time, followed by ten minutes of sudden death if the score remains level. During the sudden death period the first team to score any points is declared the winner. If no one scores in that period, the match is decided by a kicking competition. Five members of each team, who are on the field at the conclusion of the sudden death period, take place kicks from three positions on the 22-metre line. This continues until all five players from each team have kicked or until one team is unable to equal the score of the other team within the remaining number of kicks. If there are an equal number of successful kicks once each team has completed its five kicks, the competition continues on a sudden death basis, following the same order of kickers used in the first five kicks. I am hopeful for everyone's sake that we never have to go through to the kicking competition, as that would be an ugly way to win or lose.

The tournament has entered a new phase. There are no second chances—it is winner takes all. Paddy was keen to ensure that we 'referee the moment' and don't change the way we are refereeing. We don't want any surprises for the teams.

We re-affirmed various technical issues relating to player's clothing as well as discussing a few areas of play that need to be tidied up. Issues such as half-backs interfering with the scrum, foul play standards, back row binding, scrum feeds and so on. From the group's point of view everything was now planned and we were ready to play our part.

Day 27: Time off

Wednesday 3 October: It's very quiet around the hotel as the majority of the northern hemisphere guys have headed home for a couple of days before the quarter-final matches. I would love to be able to do the same but the tyranny of distance snookers me; I will have to get by with a phone call and webcam.

I made plans to catch up with Mike Heaton and the rest of the guys who are over doing the coverage with Channel Ten in their studio on the Champs Élysées. I walked into town and it was great to be able to have a good look around on my own with no time constraints.

When I arrived at the studio I met up with Mike, Scott Young (Executive Producer) and the commentary team: Bill Woods, Rupert McCall, Ben Tune and Ben Darwin. They have an incredible studio, which sits above the Champs Élysées with a 360 degree, unimpeded view of the city. They have set up the outside studio on the balcony with the Eiffel Tower as its backdrop. You can lean over and look to the right to see the Arc de Triomphe and then left to look at Place de la Concorde, I can only imagine how magical it would be at night.

They immediately congratulated me on the Wales v Fiji match and said it was a cracker and how much they had enjoyed the game and my refereeing. Scott Young was blown away by the game as they had just received the viewing figures and, despite a 1am kick off in Australia, one million viewers had watched it. He said those numbers were incredible for the time and that Channel Ten was absolutely rapt.

I answered some technical questions about our refereeing protocols such as why players had been penalised for stomping/walking on players in rucks and mauls. We also discussed dangerous tackles and what our standards were in relation to sanctions. The simple answer is that players who pick a player up are responsible for bringing them down safely and if you can't control that then don't pick them up in the first place. I know that is hard sometimes for the players but we must maintain safety as our number one priority on the field.

Mike and I left a little while later and went off to his apartment. It was fantastic to catch up with his wife Jacqui and their kids. We had a home cooked meal in a family environment and that is what I miss the most when I travel. It was a great and late night and hopefully we will do it again next week.

Day 28: A lunch to remember

Thursday 4 October: A lunch had been organised for those of us left at the hotel. We travelled to a little suburb outside Paris called Andresý where we were transported by boat to Auberge la Goelette, a wonderful restaurant located on an island on the Seine.

It often seems to be that the events that are planned at the last minute end up as the most memorable. On this occasion we were treated to some of the finest hospitality you could imagine, and it became one of those rugby highlights that I will remember forever.

The restaurant was a family-owned business who wished to host the tournament referees. Marius and his family were so generous and allowed us to share the best of French hospitality, wine and food. We were treated to a number of bottles of Möet & Chandon champagne and then we sat down to a four-course meal. We sampled some of the finest wines from various regions of the country with a vintage St-Emilion red amongst the pick. There was a lot of singing and plenty of stories and laughs.

Two emotional moments summed up the feeling of the afternoon. Paddy O'Brien had brought some signed referee jerseys along to present to our hosts Maurice, his father Pirrot and Maurice's cousin Didier. Paddy presented Pirrot with his jersey and you could see that he was deeply touched by the tears in Maurice's eyes. They put on the jerseys to a rousing cheer and ovation. It was our turn next and Nigel Owens sang a Welsh hymn called 'Mi Glywaf Dyner Lais'. As usual, his voice was incredible and nobody spoke while he sang. This hymn basically tells a story about finding the Lord and you could tell it was an emotional song for Nigel. Yet another wonderful afternoon and evening.

Day 29: Travel to Cardiff

Friday 5 October: We all feel a sense of anticipation as we are scheduled to head to Cardiff this morning for the quarter-final match between

New Zealand and France. My experience of previous tournaments is that this can be the slowest period, as you have limited travel and all matches are on the weekend.

Jonathan Kaplan, Stephen Hilditch, Bob and Eva Francis and I were due to travel together, with Stephen reviewing the match as a selector. On the flight to Cardiff Jonathan and I chatted about a number of match scenarios, various laws and touch judging, as he was keen to make sure that his preparation was on track. I also had a look at the procedures for play after a drawn match.

After such a long time in France it was great to be back in an English speaking environment for a while. Even though we are meant to be athletes I never miss the opportunity to head to Caroline Street, better known as 'Chip Alley', when I am in Cardiff. They serve the good old-fashioned thick potato chips that I used to eat as a child. It is always a great pleasure to add salt and vinegar and enjoy a 'real' chip. Travel gets you into some strange habits.

I caught up with my great mate David Hughes-Lewis over a quick beer in a local pub. It was crowded with visiting New Zealanders and locals, and a few of whom wanted to have a quiet word about the previous week when Wales had been bundled out. It was all good-natured banter—they came across and told me that it was all my fault and of course they had big smiles on their faces and were only joking. The Welsh are just fantastic supporters with a great sense of humour and these light-hearted moments are a wonderful part of rugby culture.

With all the talk in the pub, even at this stage you could sense the match tomorrow was going to be a massive occasion.

In the evening we had an informal dinner hosted by Bob Yeman, a former Welsh Test referee and now Referee Manager. As always he and his wife Chris were superb hosts and great company.

Day 30: Watching Australia v England
No 4 official, New Zealand v France

Saturday 6 October: A morning meeting began the day with Wayne Barnes (England) to go over various aspects of teamwork for the match. This is Wayne's first RWC and to be selected to referee this quarter-final match is both a great honour and well deserved. As usual, these meetings are an opportunity to confirm the way the team will work, discuss any specific issues the referee would like each person to look at, and go over communication techniques. Usually there are three ways that things can go wrong: human error, communication error or system failure. At this meeting we aim to lessen the possibility of at least two of those points occuring.

I walked around Cardiff and the atmosphere was electric with supporters dressed in their team colours enjoying the festive mood and the bars. It was a nice way to relax and pass a bit of time until we watched Australia play England.

Tony Spreadbury, his wife Pippa and Chris White joined me in my room to watch the match. I had to endure Spreaders singing 'Sweet Chariot' after the final whistle. If you were Australian it was a great disappointment but in the end you cannot deny the mental strength of England and the way they just dug in and had a go.

Like all games in this knockout stage they are won and lost by the teams who can handle the mental pressure. The sad fact is there is no tomorrow for one team. Unfortunately for Australia they had an off day and just didn't fire and I am certainly not taking anything away from England as it was a fine and well deserved win. They beat Australia's scrum and were very cagey in the way they tactically and mentally set about dismantling its foundations—this had a flow-on effect of psychologically destabilising the team.

The Australian players were confronted with a seasoned and street smart front row that used all its experience and unfortunately for the Australian scrum they couldn't match that. Any ball they got was not great quality and put pressure on the team. England slowly strangled Australia and took their opportunity to kick for points and also field position and even though Australia threatened, with Lote Tuqiri scoring a wonderfully worked try and Stirling Mortlock continually challenging the line and making breaks, the England defence held on. This frustrated Australia and things just didn't work for them.

It was a great victory for England and it was a sad sight to see the tears of Larkham and Latham and to see how shattered all the guys were. The rugby world would not see the likes of Larkham and Gregan again,

Left: *The calm before the storm—checking out the grounds before the Wales v Fiji match.*

Centre: *After the Wales v Fiji match, relaxing with a beer with touch judges Simon McDowell (Ireland) and Kelvin Deaker (New Zealand).*

Bottom: *At the Channel Ten sports headquarters in Paris. I'm on the right with, (from left) Rupert McCall, Bill Woods and Ben Tune.*

Winger Lote Tuqiri scores the first try for Australia during the Australia v England match on 6 October 2007 in Marseilles.

The Fijian team perform their Haka before the start of the quarter-final match with South Africa in Marseille on 7 October 2007.

Top: *With Paul Honiss (New Zealand, on my right) before his world record 45th Test match at the third and fourth play-off at Parc de Princes. With us are (from left) Marius Jonker (South Africa), Chris White (England), Franck Tabanelli (physiotherapist, France) and Wayne Barnes (England).*

Centre: *RWC 2007 final match ball.*

Bottom: *At the Heineken Bar with Ben Darwin, Eddie Jones and former French international player Thierry Lacroix on my right.*

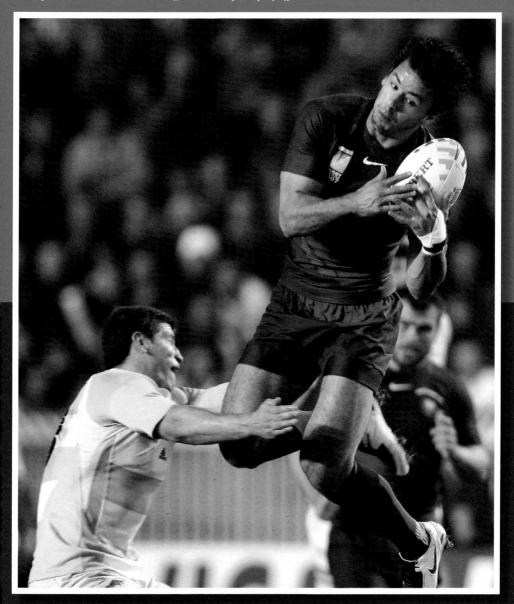

Right: *Early relaxation in the Television Match Official box at the RWC 2007 final before making one of the toughest decisions of my career so far.*

Bottom: *Too close to call for Joel Jutge (France).*

Right: 'Out, No Try'. *England's winger Mark Cueto's left foot touches the line prior to grounding the ball during the final match with South Africa at the Stade de France in Paris on 20 October 2007. Referee Alain Rolland asked me to make the call.*

Top: *Prince William and Prince Harry react to the action during the Rugby World Cup 2007 Final between England and South Africa.*

Bottom: *John Smit of South Africa lifts the trophy as his teammates celebrate victory in the 2007 Rugby World Cup Final against England.*

both of whom have been magnificent ambassadors for Australian and world rugby.

We met as a group and walked to the stadium. The roads had been closed to cars and the scenes outside our hotel were amazing with massive numbers of French fans singing the 'Marseillaise'. Millennium Stadium has to be the best in the world as the atmosphere both inside and out is unbelievable. Supporters spill out of every bar and the ground is located right in the middle of the city. The supporters are always friendly and when we are noticed we have a bit of a chat and a laugh. It is one of the greatest parts of our game that we have managed to maintain this ability to mix with the public and enjoy the spirit of rugby.

The roof of the stadium was closed and the sight looking out from the middle is one that I will always treasure. My first glimpse of the teams was when they entered the tunnel before walking on. Intense is not a good enough word to explain the feelings that were on show. You could sense the focus of both teams and the stares between players were incredible.

I leant over to Tony Spreadbury and whispered that it was 'game on here' and he smiled and nodded. The anthems were sung with such passion, the atmosphere was electric and the crowd could sense this was going to be BIG. The French went straight to halfway and stood arm in arm to face the *Haka*. It was a magnificent spectacle and I was standing only a few metres away.

The rivalry, the respect, the challenge, the acceptance, the intensity and the noise were about as good as it can get at the elite level.

It was a furious and physical start. Within a couple of minutes Serge Betsen (France) was knocked out when he attempted a tackle. It was a sickening sight to see his body hanging like a limp rag doll when he was rolled onto his side and treated by the doctors. He eventually came to and amazingly had the courage to stand and walk from the field. I think he was trying to send a message of courage to his mates. France had selected a big kicking flyhalf and fullback and in the early stages they kicked the ball back to New Zealand in an effort to tire them from running it back as well as putting pressure on by following through.

The match ebbed and flowed with lots of attack and great defence. The crowd noise was amazing and the atmosphere was incredible. The sound resonating through the closed stadium is so loud and so special. New Zealand scored a penalty goal and then the first try of the match and the place just erupted. The match then went from end to end and was a thoroughly absorbing contest. New Zealand looked in control and went into halftime with a 13–3 lead.

We went straight to our change room and the microphones on Wayne's gear were turned off so the guys could have a chat about how things were going and what we might expect in the second half. It was obviously going to be a close contest. Tim Hayes (Wales) our No 5 official and I made sure the guys had their drinks and were OK to go.

Early in the second half, Luke McAlister (New Zealand) was sent to the sin bin for an 'intentional infringement' when he pushed an attacking player thereby stopping him from supporting a teammate.

New Zealand was able to hold France out until the last seconds of the ten-minute period when they finally conceded a try. The French supporters went crazy and as I ran out to Wayne with a water bottle I couldn't hear him speak from one metre away.

France was back in the game and their supporters were really beginning to get behind them. The game moved about and the defence of both teams was incredible, however France was awarded a penalty and they were successful with the kick enabling them to tie the score at 13-13. The rolling maul and 'pick and drive' became the main weapon for both sides. Eventually, New Zealand were able to convert long periods of sustained pressure with a try that took them to a 18-13 lead. France were not spent however, and managed to come back with a try of their own from a long sweeping movement that started near halfway. The try was converted and that took them into the lead 20-18.

The last 15 minutes was as tense a rugby match as you can get. New Zealand attacked through the backs and then through the forwards with the 'pick and drive' game. France was steady as a rock and defended well. New Zealand just could not make a way through and you could sense the tide was turning and France was gaining the upper hand.

I looked across at the New Zealand bench towards the end and you could see that all sense of hope was disappearing. In contrast, the French bench was animated and it was obvious something special was happening. The contest at ruck and maul time had been huge, with New

Zealand losing possession six times and France seven. In general play, New Zealand had made nine turnovers to France's two. New Zealand passed the ball an amazing 190 times to France's 67. New Zealand had 67 per cent possession to France's 33 per cent. The ball-in-play time was a world record with it showing a figure of 57 per cent or roughly 43 minutes. Compared to the RWC 1995 statistic where the ball-in-play time was 33 per cent, it is a massive increase and a testament to the quality of both teams.

The final whistle sounded and France had won an epic and intense quarter-final. It was smiles all round for the French and tears and despair for the New Zealand team.

We went down to the change room and congratulated Wayne on what had been a great match and a contest of epic proportions. He was mentally shattered and I knew how he felt, as I was the same after the Wales v Fiji game the week before.

Paddy O'Brien came to offer congratulations to Wayne and the referee team. The police had closed the roads to normal traffic and of course there were still plenty of supporters around. So instead of having to walk back, Tony, who is still a part-time paramedic, spoke to one of his fellow paramedics. We were soon piling into the back of an ambulance and being escorted back to the hotel. There were many amused faces and comments as the six of us emerged from the back of the ambulance. It had been an amazing weekend with both Australia and New Zealand knocked out. The upsets at this tournament have been huge.

Day 31: Touch judge, Argentina v Scotland

Sunday 7 October A very early start to the day with a 7.30am pick-up from our Cardiff hotel. All of us were really tired, with only five hours' sleep. Luckily, Joel Jutge, the referee for tonight's match, had been in Paris all weekend and was well rested.

We arrived at our Paris hotel and had just enough time to go out for a quick lunch before the South Africa v Fiji quarter-final began. I watched the first 20 minutes then had a quick sleep so I would be fresh for tonight's match.

The referee team and all the others attending tonight's match met in the foyer and we left as a convoy of three cars at 6.30pm with yet another police escort. The traffic was quite heavy for a Sunday but we had the 'angry ant' leading and he managed to kick and hit a few cars along the way so we made good time to the ground.

Chris White was the other touch judge, Jonathan Kaplan was television match official (TMO) and Wayne Barnes and Tony Spreadbury were the No 4 and No 5 officials. We all went for a walk onto the pitch. There were a number of players from both teams having a walk and a chat to each other. This was a very relaxed atmosphere compared to what we had encountered the night before in Cardiff. I had a chat to Nathan Hines and Daniel Parks who are two guys who grew up and played rugby in Australia before moving overseas and qualifying for Scotland through parental ties.

We attended both dressing rooms to check the studs and clothing. The atmosphere in both camps was understated and not as hyped as last night.

When the teams walked out the stadium was full and the crowd was noisy but nothing over the top. I wondered how the match would turn out. From the opening whistle it was a dour affair with sparse intervals of open play. The main play was tight rolling mauls, 'pick and drive' and kicks for field position. Argentina scored their only try of the match from a charge down in the first half and relied on penalty and field goals. The crowd and the noise generated for this match was just at the other end of the spectrum compared to Cardiff.

There was plenty of endeavour and willingness to win but the game plans were pretty basic and it seemed the teams were of playing not to lose as opposed to trying to win. The second half was more of the same and the game and the crowd only really came alive in the final ten minutes when Scotland managed to score and Chris Paterson converted, keeping his 100 per cent kicking record for the tournament, to bring Scotland within a converted try of winning the match.

It seemed as though Argentina had gone to sleep but this managed to wake them. Scotland was trying to put pressure on but they managed to lose possession and turn the ball over too many times. On the last play of the night their lock was tackled and dropped the ball. That was the end of their tournament. The Argentinean players were ecstatic. They had taken another step forward with progression to a semi-final against South Africa.

It had been a crazy weekend with upset results and close games and now the tournament had gone from eight teams to four. It was back to the hotel to try and get some sleep and see what tomorrow would bring with selections for the last four matches.

DAY 31: 7 October 2007	
Quarter-final—Marseilles	
South Africa	37
Fiji	20

Quarter-final—Saint-Denis	
Argentina	19
Scotland	13

V.

The Semi-finals

Day 32: Selections for the finals

Monday 8 October: This is without doubt either the greatest or the worst day of a referee's tournament. The selectors were meeting to appoint the four referees for the semi-finals, third v fourth place play-off and the final.

The selectors met at 3pm and we were then scheduled to come together as a group at 4.30pm for the announcement. We duly attended but were told by Paddy O'Brien that a few phone calls needed to be made and the announcements would be made at 5pm. Taizo Hirabayshi, a Japanese referee, made a presentation to each of us on behalf of the Japan Rugby Union (JRU). We each received a commemorative RWC whistle that had been commissioned by the JRU. As we were all leaving Paddy asked me to stay for a moment to have a word. It was then I knew that the worst news was to come.

Paddy, David Pickering (Chairman of the Referees Selection Panel) and I went into another room. They said that I had refereed extremely well, done my very best and had not put a foot wrong in any of the games. The selection panel had all agreed this was the case. They told me it was a very difficult and long process and that I was right in the frame but unfortunately they had had to make a decision and it had not gone my way. They wanted to let me know before the announcement. It was a very tough moment but I appreciated their candour and immediately thanked them for taking the time to do it this way.

I returned to my room to have a few quiet moments before attending the meeting. I had prepared myself for the possibility of not being selected, but at the same time I hoped that my three performances, culminating in the Wales v Fiji match, may get me over the line. I was just so disappointed and rightly so—any person who is in any competitive environment should feel this way otherwise they don't belong. The overriding factor was that I was not going to sulk about it and I certainly was not going to walk around with my head down and withdraw from the team. I had set myself a goal and I had surpassed that goal—I had not given them a reason not to pick me and that was all I could control. I looked forward to my one-on-one meeting with the selectors to see where I could make any further improvements. One of my favourite quotes is from a speech by Reverend Martin Luther King Jr: 'The ultimate measure of a man is not where he stands in moments of comfort and convenience, but where he stands at times of challenge and controversy.' I thought this was very apt.

I headed down to the meeting. Paddy thanked us and said that he and the IRB were proud of everyone and that all of the referees had done a great job over the quarter-final week. David Pickering added that we had all performed extremely well and that this group was the best in the world and not to forget that, as everyone was a winner in the room and sometimes selection just doesn't go your way.

David announced that Jonathan Kaplan would referee England v France and Steve Walsh would referee the other semi-final between

South Africa and Argentina. Paul Honiss would referee the third v fourth play-off match and he would then become the world record holder for greatest number of Test matches refereed. David then announced that Alain Rolland would referee the RWC final. Everyone then gave a round of applause and we all congratulated each referee. I was sitting next to Alain and he just put his hands in his head and was overcome with emotion as the enormity of the appointment struck him. I congratulated him and wished him all the best for the match.

What a time of highs and lows. I was sincerely happy for all the guys. The Six Nations' appointments were then announced and I was picked for the England v Ireland match at Twickenham in March 2008.

I sent off the obligatory texts and emails to let people know what had transpired in the meeting. It was really hard to tell Fiona as I felt as though I had let her and the kids down. I had spent so much time preparing and had been away not only for this two-month period but also for long periods over the last four years leading up to the tournament. I knew deep down that the important thing was that I had done my best and that was all she had wanted me to do, but she has made so many sacrifices. I also thought of Dad and the rest of my family and friends and I knew that they would have been proud of what I had achieved.

I had my one-on-one meeting with the selectors and they were glowing in their praise of my performance during the tournament and restated that selection had been close. We talked about the future and they said if I kept my performances at the same level as I had achieved at the RWC then I would be in the frame for continued selection and higher honours. I love a challenge and, provided things don't impact on the family too much, I am back on the treadmill for the next four-year cycle to see if I can be selected again in 2011 and then see if my best will get me any higher that time.

Day 33: The day after

Tuesday 9 October: I didn't have the world's greatest sleep. I was feeling pretty flat when I woke. I decided just to get on with it and reminded myself that there were other people in the world with greater issues than mine. How true that was became obvious when I got a message from my brother saying that Mum had been taken to hospital with chest pains and an erratic heartbeat. Life has a funny way of showing you what is really important at times.

I rang the hospital and spoke to Mum. She told me she was feeling a lot better but would have some tests tomorrow and would see the cardiologist shortly. She said that she was sorry that I had not been given another game but she and the family were very proud of me for what I had achieved. My brother and sister said they would let me know how Mum is going which is a great relief—you feel pretty helpless when you are on the other side of the world.

I received a massive number of emails and texts from my family, friends and the referee fraternity with offers of condolence and support. It reminded me how lucky I was to be here and to have such a good support network. I rang Fi to tell her about Mum and it was really great to hear her voice and have a talk with the kids. It re-emphasised the real priorities in life and suddenly life seemed much better again. One of my best mates, Wayne Borland, also rang me to see how I was and that call came just at the right time.

I had some lunch with Chris White, Tony Spreadbury and Jonathan Kaplan. Chris was in the same boat as me, having found out that he was not refereeing any more matches. We agreed that there was a feeling of loss or desolation involved. The guys were very supportive and I really appreciated that support and time together. I went for a long walk in the afternoon and then trained at the gym so that I could release a bit of tension. It helped me put it all into perspective.

I had a chat with Wayne Barnes to offer my support as he was copping a fair of stick in the press about aspects of his performance, such as a missed forward pass and the sin binning of a New Zealand player in the New Zealand v France quarter-final. When teams lose there are always numerous, faceless, nameless cowards who hide behind a computer pseudonym and spew forth with their diatribes attacking individuals in a most vindictive and personal way. I, like a number of my colleagues, have been in that boat. Unfortunately, it is a sad reflection on some parts of our society that some people who have neither the courage or ability to place themselves in a position of authority or accountability suddenly allow themselves to be the judge and the jury and focus on just one piece of the pie.

Paddy O'Brien was quoted in the press fully supporting Wayne and calling for some perspective in relation to the overall picture and I thought that his stance was both sensible and necessary in order to achieve a balance in the argument. Wayne is a terrific referee and person and nobody deserves to be subjected to such appalling cowardly attacks.

Day 34: A quiet reflection

Wednesday 10 October: I spoke with Mum again this morning and all was fine—the cardiologist was very happy with her test results. A stress test will be done tomorrow and I will phone her to see how that goes.

I had a very quiet day and took the opportunity to reflect on the tournament, my matches and the many wonderful times we have had. My overall feeling is one of great satisfaction at having been involved and doing my best. I have been very privileged to be in this position. So many people have helped and made sacrifices along the way, the greatest being my wife Fiona and my kids.

It has been a great festival of rugby. The rise of the second-tier teams or 'minnows' has been fantastic for the game and the tournament and the amazing underdog wins by Argentina in the opening match and then those of the French and English teams in the quarter-finals could not have been scripted any better. It has added another dimension to a plot that has had twists and turns at every corner.

The Georgian team did so well in their matches and the Tongan boys played well above their weight to push teams to the limit. The Fijians were the pick of the 'minnow' sides, with their performances culminating in their magnificent win against Wales and then a splendid effort in the quarter-final against South Africa. The great thing this has done is to re-affirm the unpredictable nature of sport as well as show that there is still a lot more to professional sport than just money and resources. The disciplines required at this level are of course paramount to success but these minnow teams have shown that good old-fashioned pride and passion combined with skill make a very nice recipe for success. I can't wait to see what the next four years brings as these teams strive to improve even more.

Day 35: Over-inflated balls

Thursday 11 October: It was great relief to find out this morning that Mum's 'stress test' showed no major problems and that she will be fine.

I had chats with Jonathan Kaplan, Alan Lewis, Tony Spreadbury and Chris White about the upcoming semi-finals. We wondered how large the television audience would be for the England v France match. There had been reports that 16 million viewers in France alone had tuned into the France v New Zealand match and now they had '*le crunch*' to watch this weekend. I am sure the IRB and the tournament sponsors would be licking their lips in anticipation.

We had a bit of a laugh about the press reports about the match balls being used at the tournament. This has been an ongoing saga with the teams and kickers having had 'problems' with the match balls supposedly being different to those used at training. The latest 'answer' to the missed kicks was that the balls were over-inflated and the scientists had showed that this would affect the flight of the ball. A couple of the journalists had then dragged out players of the past to run a few classic 'in my day' stories about how you 'just kicked the damn thing', and of course this was followed with the obligatory 'these blokes in the professional era are pampered' line. Oh to be the editor of a newspaper with a thousand angles to run with! I made myself a mental note to chat to Jonny Wilkinson on Saturday before the match to find out exactly what he thought from his so-called 'pampered' position.

Later on I caught up with friends from Sydney; Maurice Doria and his wife Tammy, their kids Hayden and Antony, Tammy's Mum and Maurice's sister. It was fantastic to get into that family environment and have a chat, as well as home-cooked roast beef with vegetables.

Day 36: On the panel at Channel Ten

Friday 12 October: It is a day away from the semi-final weekend and the hotel has become really busy with tour groups booking in. Many of these groups are full of dejected Kiwis that have paid their money and don't have a team to support. I suppose you could say that about the Aussies all over France as well.

Tony Spreadbury and I are TMOs for the semi-finals and we went through the relevant procedures, protocol and laws just to ensure we are up to speed. Tony will be retiring from international refereeing at the end of the tournament and I will miss him. He is a first class gentleman, great referee and a wonderful servant of the game. I know he will leave the game with many great memories and achievements.

In the afternoon, I went to the Channel Ten studios on the Champs Élysées to be part of their panel show. Eddie Jones, former Wallaby coach, and Thierry Lacroix, former French international player, were also guests. Eddie was in great spirits and obviously enjoying his time with the South African team. We talked about the Australian and New Zealand teams being knocked out. He was really disappointed for the Australians as they had played a poor game and that would be hardest thing for them to come to terms with. There was no doubt that England deserved to win and there were no excuses. It was wonderful to meet Thierry, as I had watched him play as a flyhalf for France and I had always thought he was a class player. He is moving to Sydney as his wife is Australian and he is really looking forward to the new start.

The panel asked me about refereeing issues and my games. I couldn't answer some questions, as the IRB didn't want me commenting on certain aspects relating to match officials. There was some discussion about the touch judge's role in calling incidents to help the referees. They were specifically interested in the 'missed' forward pass in the New Zealand v France quarter-final and while I couldn't comment specifically on the matter I could explain the role of the touch judge. I was able to answer that if a touch judge sees something that is clear and obvious then they should call it, but you have to ensure that it is clear and obvious and not a guess or balance of probability. I managed to sidestep some of the lines of questioning and the guys were good about it, as they didn't apply any pressure.

We had a bit of a laugh at the expense of Chris White and Jonathan Kaplan, as they played footage of them being knocked over in their games. Finally, we had a segment with Ben Darwin, Eddie, Thierry and myself standing at the Heineken Bar answering a few questions.

I headed off to catch up with Wayne Erickson, former Australian Test referee, and his wife Debra. Along the way I was stopped by a couple of South Africans who recognised me and wanted to talk about the RWC. I always make time for the supporters if they want to talk, as it is just as interesting for me to find about rugby from their perspective.

I ran into former Wallaby players Richard Harry, David Wilson and Jason Little. They were in fine form and looked as though they were still fit enough to play. I finally made it to see Wayne and Debra and we went back to their apartment to have a home-cooked meal.

Day 37: TMO, France v England

Saturday 13 October: The day started with a team meeting led by Paddy O'Brien to review logistics and refocus the group on maintaining our standards. Obviously the stakes are higher with the semi-finals this weekend and the final the week after. We reconfirmed the touch judge roles and looked at some video clips to ensure that we were all still in sync with our primary (touch), secondary (foul play) and tertiary (any other assistance) roles. We also restated our position about only making calls on matters that are clear and obvious. This was a useful session in re-affirming our roles and focusing on our tasks.

I had a chat to Jonathan Kaplan, tonight's referee, to see how he was feeling about the match. He was probably as focused as I had ever seen him before a game.

We arrived at the ground at 7pm and went out to the field to have a look and take some photographs. The English team came out shortly after and a few of the guys wandered past and had a chat. Phil Vickery, the English captain, came over towards me and I wished him all the best. He said that the team was ready but he was worried because they had the best training session of the tour on Thursday and he hoped they hadn't left their form on the training paddock rather than producing it at match time.

He was half joking, but players are always wary of that scenario because you can create a false confidence by thinking you are well prepared and as a result don't focus as well and thereby lose that 1 per cent that can mean the difference between winning and losing the tight matches.

I had also had a chat to John Kirwan, former New Zealand player and current coach of Japan, who was commentating for Italian TV. He was in the middle of contract negotiations with Japan as well as being dismayed with New Zealand's loss. Christophe Dominici, the French winger, also stopped and said hello. He is a terrific fellow and a great player and I have formed a really good relationship with him, as we have shared a few drinks together at various after-match functions.

I went up to find the TMO box and saw the television producer to make sure we agreed on my calls to him for replays. I asked to see the camera angles from the end of the ground and from one side it was perfect with a view up the touchline. On the other side part of my view was cut off if the player went any deeper than 1–1.5 metres in goal. I checked whether they could be moved and was told no, so I just hoped that nothing came down that side.

The TMO box has a thick glass window and the noise of the crowd is quite muffled so you don't get the same appreciation of the atmosphere. However despite the glass, when both teams came out, with Jason Robinson leading England for his fiftieth Test, the noise was amazing and I could only wonder how loud it actually was in the stadium. The anthems were sung and the teams lined up ready for the kick off. We did a final sound check and I wished Jonathan all the best.

The English were to celebrate very quickly when at one minute 12 seconds Josh Lewsey followed a kick by Andy Gomarsall. The French fullback, Damien Traille, was too casual and let the ball bounce, it sat up for Lewsey who jumped above Traille and caught it and fell over the line to score. This was about as close as I came to being used in the match; sometimes that just happens whereas in other matches you may get a number of calls. Wilkinson converted and it was 7–0.

France looked shell-shocked. The rest of the half was an arm wrestle with both teams playing the mauling game with 'pick and drive' as well as looking for field position with tactical kicking.

The mentality in these big matches is for players not to make mistakes in their own half. They will usually play a pattern that is designed to put pressure on the other side. In this case, both teams were kicking and occasionally chancing their arm by having a run. It was a close contest. France lost their inspirational lock, Fabien Pelous, to a rib injury about 20 minutes into the first half, which meant that the French crowd favourite, Sébastien Chabal, came on to a rousing chorus of cheers. It also meant that France were without the same direction that Pelous's experience could give. Lionel Beauxis was able to kick two penalty goals while Wilkinson missed one from halfway. Both kickers attempted and missed drop goals and France went into half time with a 6–5 lead.

The second half was more of the same tactics. Perhaps France should have run with the ball more as their kicking game was not tactically as good as the English. Both teams tried to put pressure on the other by kicking long for field position and then pressuring for a penalty or a mistake that may lead to quick turnover ball and an opportunity to score.

France went further ahead, 9–5, with a penalty from Beauxis. A couple of minutes later Wilkinson also scored a penalty goal to make it 9–8 to France. Substitutions were made and France put on Michelak at flyhalf to open up the game to France's advantage. The crowd was growing louder with the English singing 'Swing Low' and the French shouting 'Allez les Bleus' or breaking into their national anthem. It was great theatre and added to the occasion. Wilkinson attempted a drop goal that hit the post and after more attack by England, France was able to kick the ball away and relieve pressure. France then had an opportunity and kicked over the try line. It was easily caught in goal and was wasted possession and opportunity. From the drop out France attacked with a cross kick that was beautifully knocked back to a support player and had he not been ankle tapped by a desperate England defender he would have scored. He instead fell to the ground and was stopped.

France then had a five-metre scrum and an opportunity to attack. They turned over this ball after good defence by England and you could see this was a moment that defined the match for England.

It was then more kicking for field position from both teams. As France was in the lead the pressure was on England. England received a penalty for a high tackle and Wilkinson converted. Suddenly England was in the lead 11–9. The English supporters were ecstatic and the noise I could hear through Jonathan's microphone was incredible. France now had to attack as they were behind. England soaked up the pressure and eventually made their way down field with rolling mauls. Jonny Wilkinson kicked a field goal to put them further ahead 14–9.

As a TMO you are also the timekeeper and it was my job to let Jonathan know the time left at 20 minutes, five minutes and two minutes. Finally, when time has expired you call 'in your time' so the referee knows that this is the last play.

I called 'in your time' to Jonathan and there was no response. France was attacking and it should have been all over at the next stoppage. I was hoping that the system did not fail now, as it would have been an amazing scene if he had played on again after a stoppage because he could not hear me. I tried twice more and thankfully he eventually he heard me as a stoppage occurred almost immediately after. It was full-time and England was through to the final to defend the RWC. While it was not a classic game it was a tense match and the fans and players from both teams looked exhausted.

DAY 37: 13 October 2007	
Semi-final—Saint-Denis	
France	9
England	14

Day 38: Watching South Africa v Argentina

Sunday 14 October: I was not appointed an official for this match and that meant I had a free day. I caught up on some emails and visited some friends. I caught up with Mick Keogh, Australian National Referee Coach, and his wife Maureen. We parked ourselves at a small café on the Champs Élysées and ran into former Wallaby prop Fletcher Dyson and his wife Mandy. Fletch retired only a couple of years ago due to a neck injury. Given the fact that he, Ben Darwin, Brendan Cannon and others had finished due to injury or retirement then it is understandable why the Australian front row stocks do not have a huge amount of combined Test experience.

Fletch is now the scrum coaching guru for the new Melbourne-based team in the Australian Rugby Championship. He was quite excited about the new competition and how it provided a genuine step-up from club rugby. He thought this would help Australian rugby by testing players in a pressured playing environment.

Mick, Maureen and I went for a walk and then grabbed some lunch. We caught up on all the refereeing matters and how things had progressed for me at the tournament and we were both extremely happy that all the plans we had developed had worked, as I had achieved great results in all my games. Mick has always been a great coach in the way that he challenges my thinking and refereeing and is always striving to ensure that I continue to improve and learn.

I headed back to the hotel to watch the South Africa v Argentina semi-final. Not being at the game was different, but I actually enjoyed just sitting and relaxing in a comfortable environment as it allowed me to feel like a normal spectator.

The South Africans went into this semi-final as legitimate favourites but one can never predict the results, given the last two weekends. The Argentineans adopted a basic game plan throughout the tournament. They kicked for field position, put pressure on their opponents and waited to seize opportunities that may arise from forcing teams into mistakes. In this game they suddenly and surprisingly adopted an open approach and this led to all of South Africa's four tries.

Fourie du Preez and Bryan Habana scored intercept tries and the other two came from quick turnover balls where Argentina made unforced errors. Bryan Habana scored a wonderful solo try when the ball was thrown wide very quickly after a turnover. Habana then chipped over the top and regathered to run in from 30 metres out. He is so quick; it was a terrific piece of well-finished counterattack.

The South Africans have a wonderful lineout so the Argentineans were reluctant to kick the ball out as it would mean giving away possession. This led to a different type of tactical kicking with high bombs and long raking kicks downfield. South Africa lead 24–6 at half time but they had weathered a fair amount of attack and pressure from Argentina. They probably weren't as composed as they would like to have been but they had a lead and that was all that mattered to them.

In the second half, Argentina scored early and continued to put pressure on the South African scrum and at the breakdown. They could not turn that advantage into anything positive and crucially did not score more points. The South Africans gave away a number of penalties and the Argentine captain, Gus Pichot, let his frustration get the better of him and was penalised for foul play when his team was in a great position to mount more pressure and attack.

This was the story of the night with Argentina losing the composure that had held them in good stead throughout the tournament. South Africa soaked up the pressure and converted their chances into points. At the final whistle South Africa won the match 37–13—they had made the final for the first time since 1995 when they won on home soil. It was the end for a gallant Argentina who had done what many thought impossible and reached the final four. You could see the heartache and sadness that the loss caused and this was compounded by the fact that the majority of this team would retire from international rugby and had lost their chance at winning the World Cup. It would now be interesting to see who can pick themselves up for the third v fourth play-off match the following Friday.

Depending on how you like your rugby there are two distinct camps. The first are those who want to see tries and action all the time and find a 12–6 scoreline with penalty goals unacceptable. On the other hand, there are those that think that free flowing rugby is to be frowned on. I just like to see a contest and one style can be as good as the other. This weekend we had two different matches that saw a lot of kicking and some stifled play as well as passages of great movement and that adds to the whole occasion to create that theatre and drama that is the hallmark of sport. England v France had the crowd on the edge of their seat due to a close score and twists and turns where any mistake could be costly and Argentina v South Africa provided a different contrast where one team just took opportunities and soaked up the pressure.

DAY 38: 14 October 2007	
Semi-final—Saint-Denis	
South Africa	37
Argentina	13

VI.

The Play-off and Final

Day 39: Finals' appointments

Monday 15 October: The selectors met this morning to finalise the remaining appointments for the final and the third v fourth play-off matches. I was appointed as the reserve referee and touch judge for the third v fourth play-off and TMO for the final.

A lot of the guys were talking about the TMO being a poison chalice, as I may have to make a decision that could determine the final result. I have no trouble with that. Of course I would rather be refereeing the final, who wouldn't, but I take the view that at least I would get to see a number of replays and have a bit of time to look at something, whereas on the ground you only have a split second. I love a challenge anyway. I guess I could always hope that I am not asked to make any calls but decision-making is what I am trained to do. I look forward to being involved in the matches and supporting the referees.

A group of us headed of to a wine tasting exhibition that was being held as part of the Rugby World Cup celebrations. We were treated to a wonderful lunch and provided with many wines to taste during and after the meal. We were also honoured with an appearance by the world's number one wine-taster or sommelier, Mr Philippe Faure-Brac. It was terrific fun and nice way to spend an afternoon.

Day 40: Team dinner

Tuesday 16 October: We are all now waiting for the weekend's matches. I have to prepare for my role as a touch judge and a possible referee should Paul Honiss have any problems on Friday night. Paul will become the world record holder with 45 Test matches and I certainly don't want him to come off but we must prepare for all possibilities.

It will be very interesting to see how the teams play and in fact what players they choose as there is always talk that this third place play-off is a waste of time as the players really don't want to be there. However I am sure that France will want to win in order to give something back to the nation. On the other hand, Argentina will see third place as a huge achievement and more evidence that they should play regularly in a big tournament like the Six Nations or Tri-Nations.

I spent the afternoon with Chris White and we went to the Army Museum at Hôtel des Invalides and saw Napoleon's Tomb and the World War I and World War II exhibition. We chatted about the tournament and how well it had been run. He really wants England to win the final again—I think he just wants another invitation to Buckingham Palace. We also discussed the new experimental laws. There have been a lot of press articles about the tournament being full of kicking and how some of the games have been poor spectacles. Supposedly the new laws will speed up the game. It will be interesting to see how this unfolds when the IRB debate the data coming in from all over the world and

SANZAR trial them in the Super 14 competition.

I will be very interested to see which of the experimental rules are introduced into the Super 14 competition, as I have a Six Nations game in the middle of the Super 14 season and it will be an interesting proposition to get my head around two sets of laws. Maybe I will not referee at Super 14 until my Six Nations duties are complete.

Our referee base is the Novotel, Gare de Lyon and the staff have been truly wonderful. The General Manager arranged a dinner as a celebration of our stay and it turned out to be a great night. As a group we have been treated so well wherever we have been. Paddy made some presentations to the staff and Stephen Hilditch then made a speech on the behalf of the group to Tony Spreadbury. Tony will retire from international refereeing after the tournament and he will be greatly missed. It was an emotional moment for everybody, as gentlemen like Tony don't come along that often.

Day 41: Rest day

Wednesday 17 October: A rest day was in order after a late finish or early morning depending on how you looked at it. After lunch Wayne Barnes, Chris White and I went to the Picasso Museum. My English friends thought it was wonderful that an Australian would be interested in broadening his cultural horizons, as they continually tell me 'the only culture Australians know is yoghurt'.

Wayne has handled his stint of adverse publicity from the quarter-final really well and it has been very impressive to see him take it in his stride. As a practical joke his housemates arranged a blonde wig and fake moustache for him when they went to the England v France semi-final. When the guys went out on the Sunday night after Steve Walsh's semi-final, Walshy took them to a bar full of Kiwis and Wayne, without disguise, was introduced to people as Jimmy Barnes. Not one of the Kiwi supporters recognised him!

In the evening Chris White, Nigel Owens and I visited Brian Campsall, a former English test referee who is currently a referee coach with the English Rugby Union (RFU). Brian is over in his capacity as a consultant to the English team. He is a terrific fellow and always has a big smile on his face. It was even bigger this time as the English had made the final and disposed of the Aussie team along the way.

Although the Australian boys lost, it was really pleasing to hear him say that the English boys really rated the Aussies and use them as a bit of a litmus test as they believe that the Australian team is probably the toughest team to beat as the guys have so much heart and never lie down. As a fellow Australian that is great to hear, because if there is one thing we are proud of, that is our ability to have a go and never give up. I guess that is epitomised by our soldiers who fought so bravely in France in World War I.

It was also interesting talking to Nigel Owens as this was his first trip on the underground in Paris. We keep forgetting that he comes from a small village in Wales where some people have never been to Cardiff, let alone London.

Day 42: Train strike

Thursday 18 October: We are a day away from the third place play-off and the atmosphere around town is starting to intensify. That's if you can actually make it in to the city, as the rail unions have called a 24-hour strike. The national rail group, SNCF, happens to be a major sponsor for the tournament and I don't think they are too happy about the situation.

I spent a bit of time this morning going through some game preparation as a referee and a touch judge as I will be reserve referee tomorrow night and I have to be prepared.

One of my best mates, Wayne Borland, flew into town this morning with his brother-in-law, Lachlan. I walked up to Notre Dame to meet up with them and we wandered around the city. We managed to have a couple of cleansing ales along the way. I left them in the early evening as their jet lag set in and joined the referee group who had gone to a restaurant for dinner. This was an opportunity to catch up with Paul Honiss and tomorrow's referee team.

Having a meal together before a match is a great tradition for referees and one that we hope will never be lost to the game.

Day 43: France v Argentina play-off
for third and fourth place

Friday 19 October: The penultimate match day for the tournament beckons, with France v Argentina to see who will finish for third and fourth positions. It was a leisurely start with a late breakfast and then time to catch up with Chris White's family who had arrived on Thursday evening. I went for a walk up to Notre Dame and then on to meet up with Wayne and Lachlan as well as Douggie Hunter and his wife Carol.

Douggie is from Scotland and is here in his capacity as a citing commissioner but I have known him and Carol for many years—he was previously a lower level referee and has been involved in refereeing and judicial administration for many years. We had a quiet lunch and then it was time to squeeze back onto one of the limited metro services and make my way back to the hotel and a team meeting with Paul Honiss and Nigel Owens, who would also run touch with me in the match.

We left for the Parc de Princes at 6.30pm and the traffic was incredible because of the Metro strike. While some services had resumed, the knock on effect was disastrous and at times we were stuck in gridlock. Thank goodness for a police escort this time, as we would not have had a chance of making it anywhere near time without it.

This was a great ride as we had to spend heaps of time on the wrong side of the road with cars coming at us and while some of the guys were a bit fearful I loved it as it bought back old memories of my days driving police cars in the same situation.

When we got to the ground we went out onto the field to have a look around, take some photos and kill some time before the teams arrived and all the prematch protocols kicked in.

We went to the Argentinean change room first. They were very focused but at the same time were going about their business in a quiet and relaxed manner. Nigel and I checked the boots and padding and all was fine. They were so happy to have achieved so much but at the same time wanted to finish off on a high.

The French dressing room was a little more somber and while the guys were quiet I could feel that there was a lot more tension here. Nigel and I went through the same routine and I had a chat to Christophe Dominici. They just didn't want to let themselves or the country down. There is massive pressure for them being the home team and it must contribute in some way to their performance.

Our dressing room was very relaxed and Paul had some music playing. There was a few laughs mixed in amongst the seriousness of the occasion. We were all ready for whatever may be thrown our way and I congratulated Paul on his record Test match tonight and we all wished him the best.

The crowd of nearly 46,000 welcomed the teams with great fanfare and the teams responded with very loud and purposeful renditions of their national anthems and the crowd was then straight into the chant of 'Allez les Bleus' to psyche up their team. Paul blew the whistle and the half began. This would be forty minutes of full concentration on the touch line as we had some cantankerous players to deal with.

The French were in a sprint from the start, throwing the ball around. The crowd was alive and enthusiastic. They had three try scoring opportunities denied through over exuberance and this began to tell on them during the half where the pressure built and a number of incidents occurred.

The French had two forward passes called back and then, on my touch line, Aurelien Rougerie threw a quick line out, however, he was ahead of the mark and the throw was not allowed. I called 'no no no' into the communications gear above the noise and he saw me and stopped the play. For the sake of less than two metres and composure the French may have scored and got their tails in the air but it was not to be.

The Pumas (Argentina) contested the breakdown fiercely and tackled with great purpose. This lead to the French making handling errors which also added to their frustration. During this time we had a number of players from both teams pulling at jerseys and doing silly things to try and upset each other and get someone to lose composure and throw a punch. They traded penalty goals and then Argentina scored a try out wide to go to the lead 10–3.

The French didn't come back and the Pumas scored again. It was 17–3 with France under huge pressure. We then had a number of small skirmishes and as a touch judge I had to concentrate and scan everywhere. The French tried a number of tap kicks and could not breach the line and this frustration finally led to Paul sin binning a player from each team, one of them Raphael Ibanez, the French captain.

We went into half time with hyped up players and intense emotion. The break was a perfect opportunity for the players to calm down.

The magic water must have done the trick as the second half was a different game. As a team of three, particularly the referee, you like to think that you have contributed successfully to that change in player behaviour by your management of the action. It is all about transferring that pressure back onto the teams and two yellow cards and strong refereeing by Paul certainly did that.

The French ran early and then went into their shell again with rolling mauls and some occasional running brilliance, but it was the Pumas who changed their style and went from a kicking and mauling style, which had been their standard play for the tournament, into a running game that ended up with them scoring five tries to one in the overall match.

They kept the pressure on France, winning turnover ball and attacking from everywhere. They scored three magnificent tries. It was running rugby at its best and a sight to behold.

Their best try saw them break down the left hand side and they ended up scoring on the right with a ripper pass from the flyhalf Hernandez I was in line with it on my touch line and it was a left to right pass that must have travelled at least 20 metres. It was fast and in front of the player who ran onto it. It was perfectly executed. That is why it is great be a referee as you get a close up look at the incredible skill. It reminded me of when I ran right beside Stephen Larkham in a match when he did that and the ball was flat and there was no-one in the field of vision and then suddenly Stirling Mortlock appeared from nowhere and hit the ball and the line at full speed and was away. It was absolutely amazing to see.

In the end, the match statistics showed that while the Pumas had only 35 per cent of possession, they scored five tries to one and defended against a team that had 65 per cent of the ball. It was an amazing effort and they were deserved winners.

In a very touching moment, Paul was presented with a Test jersey by the managers of each of the teams who had come in to say thank you and also congratulate him for reaching the new world record of 45 Test matches. That was a great gesture.

Augustine Pichot, the Puma's captain, came in with his little daughter to say hi and thanks. Gus has been a great competitor and at times has also given a bit of lip to referees. He has been a wonderful player and servant of the game and can retire from international rugby with his held high after achieving so much and playing such a vital role in the rise of Argentine rugby. The only question now is whether they can make their way into one of the top tier international tournaments such as Six Nations or Tri-Nations.

DAY 43: 19 October 2007	
Third and fourth play-off—Paris	
France	10
Argentina	34

Day 44: The RWC Final:
England v South Africa and 'that TMO decision'

Saturday 20 October: The final day of the tournament has arrived. We started with a 10am meeting where Paddy O'Brien needed to sort out some last minute logistical issues and wish Alain and the referee team all the best for the match tonight. There was a good vibe amongst the guys and plenty of sledging between the English and South African guys.

Alain Rolland had organised a meeting with the two touch judges, Joel Jutge and Paul Honiss, and me to go over a few things before the match. Alain and I discussed TMO (Television Monitor Official) issues and what he would ask about tries: 'can you tell me if a try has been scored?' and 'is there any reason why I can't award a try?

We also discussed timekeeping in the match. I raised the fact that there was a language barrier with the producer and that I had experienced problems with getting the correct footage and replays when I had previously been TMO. I told him that I would be as quick as possible but any really close decisions may take some time due to these issues but I would keep him informed.

We left the hotel at 6.30pm with our final police escort. The crowds outside on the streets and in the bars around the stadium were large and noisy. It was an interesting feeling to be involved in both the opening and closing games of this RWC.

I was just as excited about this game as I was about the first, even though we have had nearly eight weeks of rugby in between.

I walked out onto the field to look at the crowd and the ground—I had two hours to kill before kick off. The numbers in the stands were slowly building. I was excited about being at another RWC final—I had been involved in 1999 and 2003. I spoke to Eddie Jones and Jake White and they were really looking forward to the contest. They said they thought it would be very physical. I spoke with Brian Ashton and as usual he had a laugh and a smile

Alain, Joel and Paul spoke to the teams and I went to see the producer to confirm the camera angles I needed and the type of replays I would require, such as slow motion or freeze frame. In the change room, the guys had come back in and they said that both teams were focused and the change rooms were deathly quiet. They expected the physicality and intensity to be incredible. We wished each other all the best and I headed off upstairs to the TMO box.

We did a sound check and all was fine so now it was a matter of sitting and waiting for the game to begin. Looking around the ground there were significantly more white shirts supporting England than there were the green shirts of South Africa. It was a spectacular sight and the atmosphere was great. After focusing on a number of the spectators I wrote a note on my paper that said, 'so much expectation and hope'.

The teams came out to great celebration and fanfare and the crowd settled down to sing the national anthems. We made our final sound checks and Alain blew the whistle and the game was underway.

The physicality and intensity was there from start to finish and while it was not the most attractive of matches, both teams gave it everything and never gave up. It was a contest of determination, spirit and will to win. The first half saw a lot of kicking for field position, with South Africa dominating the lineout by stealing a number of the English throws. Both teams' defensive lines held resolutely and the tackling was brutal at times. This English team has shown so much character to come back from a 36–0 defeat to South Africa in the pool rounds to make it to the final. They were not going to relinquish their World Cup crown without a fight.

Penalty goals were traded and after ten minutes the score was 3–3. There was more thrust and parry with some glimpses of counter attack and after 15 minutes South Africa took the lead 6–3 after a penalty was given away by England for tripping. This was not the game for either team to give away points through ill discipline.

In the final ten minutes of the first half, South Africa appeared to be getting on top and opening up the game a little. Francois Steyn was making a few midfield breaks and the pendulum was just starting to swing South Africa's way. England not giving up. though and was holding on. Percy Montgomery landed a late penalty and South Africa went to half time with a 9–3 lead.

The second half started in the same manner with kicks for field position. Near the two-minute mark South Africa dropped the ball and Matthew Tait swooped and made a wonderful break for the line. He was tackled just short and the ball was spun left and Mark Cueto dived for the line with a desperate Danie Rossouw stretching out to try and tackle him into touch.

Joel Jutge was the touch judge. Alain consulted with him and they decided to come 'upstairs' for me to adjudicate. My heartbeat went up, I stopped the clock and Alain said to me: 'Is there any reason why I cannot award a try?' I repeated the question and began looking at the monitor. I flicked the switch and called for the producer and there was no answer. The front-on replay came onto the screen so I started watching while still trying to contact the producer.

The secret to any good decision-making is process. I had done my pre-match planning and now that plan was in action. I could see quite clearly on the first replay that Mark had grounded the ball and his body was not out, however there was a question as to whether his left foot had touched the line before grounding the ball. This front-on replay at full speed was not going to help me. I needed a replay from behind. It was clear his foot was definitely near or on the touchline prior to grounding the ball. All I required was to find a replay that showed me whether his foot had clearly touched the line.

The producer gave me side on shots and eventually gave me a replay from directly behind. This was the shot I needed. By the time he got to this replay he had still not spoken to me and this was a concern, as I needed to get a slow motion shot. Eventually he came on the line and I told him I needed that shot from behind again and that I needed to freeze the picture and possibly have a slow motion shot as well.

The re-cueing of that shot took an age and when he gave it to me he did not slow it down nor did I get a freeze-frame as requested. I asked again. I kept looking at the picture while this was happening and this is why it all took so long. I kept Alain informed and I was happy that we had planned for this contingency before the match.

Eventually we got the footage from behind again and once again there was no reply from the producer. The footage was played at full speed with no freeze frame as requested and I knew that I was going to have make a decision without the help I expected. I knew that it was extremely close and in these cases our standards are clear, 'If you cannot prove it is out then it is in'.

On my next look I could see that the toe was touching the line. I looked at it one more time at full speed and I said to myself, 'skid, touch, up, down' referring to the sequence with the foot and then the grounding of the ball. It was now clear to me; I had trusted my process and not let time or the other distractions affect it. I had come up with a decision and, more importantly, a correct decision. I informed Alain that the foot was in touch and it was no try. He said thanks and awarded England a penalty from advantage for a South African infringment.

I was glad that was over, it had been a tough call and there was obvious disappointment from the English and ecstasy from the South Africans. My screen immediately showed a shot of Prince William and you could see the disappointment. He nearly said something but I think he must have thought the lip readers would make an international incident of it so he kept his mouth closed. I met him during the British and Irish Lions tour of New Zealand in 2005 and I thought 'there goes my chance of ever being knighted'.

The game rolled on with more kicking for field position and driving mauls with plenty of tension and a few glimpses of open play. Alain eventually blew full time. South Africa was the winner 15–6 and world champions for the second time.

I knew at the time my decision was crucial but just how crucial was reflected in the score at the end of the game. I was satisfied and proud that I had made the right call given the circumstances and the fact that this was the biggest game of rugby in the world in 2007.

I turned on my phone and received a phone call from my good mate David Kurk in London who said that the replays showed the call was right and that Martin Johnson, former English captain, had also agreed with my call. I was grateful for Kurky's call, as even though you know in your own mind that you are right it is always a great feeling when there is other support that takes you from 100 per cent to 200 per cent sure.

I made my way down onto the field and, because the stadium had seen the same replays as me, it was clear that some people still thought the decision was incorrect. There was no way I was going to hide so I stayed out on the field to watch the ceremony. It was quite obvious the English team was upset at the loss and that some of them thought it was a try. That was understandable given their circumstances so I just stayed at a discreet distance so as not to cause any angst or create a scene. There was a funny moment when an English supporter casually walked onto the pitch through the crowd of VIPs, such as South African President Thabo Mbeki, and picked up and kissed the World Cup before security realised he was intruder and arrested him. I congratulated Alain and he was so happy; his little boy, Mark, was brought onto the field and that added to his joy. Eventually we went back into the change room and it was congratulations all round for the referee team.

The guys said they were glad it was me making the call and not them. I received a number of phone calls and text messages of support and that was wonderful. Paddy O'Brien came in and spoke to the guys and then we had a chat and he asked me about the call and I told him what had happened and that I knew it was correct. He immediately said 'well done' and acknowledged how tough the call was. He then reiterated that was why the selectors had appointed me as TMO for the final.

We went back to the team room to celebrate. It was a great night with many speeches and votes of thanks and it was the last opportunity for us to be together as a group.

Jonathan Kaplan called me over to the computers and showed me a still picture from the BBC website that clearly showed Mark Cueto's left foot on the touch line with the ball above the ground. I immediately thought if only I had that still shot some hours ago there would have been no doubt from anyone. I felt very happy that I had backed my process, given the fact that I had to make the decision watching the reply at 'full speed'. This decision also happened to be the most crucial decision I have made so far in my refereeing career. Shortly after, Jonathan must have shown Paddy the BBC still shot as he interrupted the gathering and made a point of publicly congratulating me on a great decision.

So it's the end of my World Cup for 2007. I reflected with Jonathan Kaplan, Chris White and Tony Spreadbury and we all agreed that it had been a great team and a wonderful experience. Personally, I was just so happy that I had done all that I could have possibly done and achieved my goal of refereeing to the best of my ability.

There were two wonderful highlights from on the field. The first was refereeing that wonderful game between Wales and Fiji and the second was being involved in a match as important as the World Cup final and having to make such a crucial decision and getting it 100 per cent correct.

I had done my job well and I reflected on how I had kept my word to my father that I would make him proud of me at this tournament. I now looked forward to going home and seeing my wonderful family as

I had been away from them for two months.

I knew that now I had come to the end of a long season and I would be taking a well earned holiday and time away from rugby with Fiona and my family. The Super 14 and Six Nations in 2008 will be my next assignment, but that can wait as I look forward to a couple of months getting back to a normal homelife.

DAY 43: 20 October 2007	
Final—Saint-Denis	
England	6
South Africa	15

Day 44: Signing off

Sunday 21 October: A number of the guys have left, and those of us remaining are heading off to the IRB Awards night. Amongst other logistical duties, we handed back our tournament phones. I turned on my own personal phone, to find a message from my mate Craig Kirkland, who had been with me in the police force in the shooting incident in Pennant Hills in 1991.

The message read: 'Second time you've had a gun at your head and came out on top. Cheers mate.'